SELLING AT THE
PRO LEVEL

SELLING AT THE
PRO LEVEL

HOW TO INCREASE YOUR SALES

*BY LEARNING THE WINNING STRATEGIES & PRINCIPALS
THAT WILL PROPEL YOU TO SUCCESS*

LARRY LOCKSHAW

GREAT ACHIEVERS
Publishing

Copyright © 2018 by Larry Lockshaw

Published by Great Achievers Publishing

Email: GreatAchieversPublishing@gmail.com

All rights reserved. This book or any portion thereof may not be reproduced or used in any manner whatsoever without the express written permission of the publisher except for the use of brief quotations in a book review or scholarly journal.

No part of this publication may be reproduced, stored in a retrieval system, or transmitted in any form or by any means, electronic, mechanical, photocopying, recording, scanning, or otherwise, except as permitted under Section 107 or 108 of the 1976 United States Copyright Act, without either the prior written permission of the Publisher, or authorization through payment of the appropriate per-copy fee to the Copyright Clearance Center, Inc., 222 Rosewood Drive, Danvers, MA 01923, (978) 750-8400, fax (978) 646-8600, or on the web at www.copyright.com. Requests to the Publisher for permission should be addressed to the Permissions Department, John Wiley & Sons, Inc., 111 River Street, Hoboken, NJ 07030, (201) 748-6011, fax (201) 748-6008, or online at www.wiley.com/go/permissions.

Limit of Liability/Disclaimer of Warranty: While the publisher and author have used their best efforts in preparing this book, they make no representations or warranties with respect to the accuracy or completeness of the contents of this book and specifically disclaim any implied warranties of merchantability or fitness for a particular purpose. No warranty may be created or extended by sales representatives or written sales materials. The advice and strategies contained herein may not be suitable for your situation. You should consult with a professional where appropriate. Neither the publisher nor author shall be liable for any loss of profit or any other commercial damages, including but not limited to special, incidental, consequential, or other damages.

Printed in the United States of America.

FIRST EDITION

10 9 8 7 6 5 4 3 2 1

Selling at the PRO Level

/Larry Lockshaw

To my beautiful, gracious, God loving and dedicated wife Karen and to my brilliant son Matt who is so talented and creative.

Thank you both. Without your support and patience, I would have never achieved this dream.

"Employ your time in improving yourself by other men's writings, so that you shall gain easily what others have labored hard for."

- Socrates

TABLE OF CONTENTS

WHY I WROTE THIS BOOK...1
ACKNOWLEDGEMENTS..3
INTRODUCTION...5

Chapter 1
    From Low Level To PRO Level 7

Chapter 2
    The Results are In... And You Did Not Make
    The Top 10, Again 13

Chapter 3
    Listening to a Mentor..19

Chapter 4
    Perception is HUGE. 27

Chapter 5
    A Selling Technique
    That Will 'Blow Away' Your Customers 39

Chapter 6
    I'm sorry Mr. Customer,
    What was Your Name Again?...45

Chapter 7
    Why Am I Doing This Anyway?
    There's got to be an easier way to make a living...Right?........49

Chapter 8
    Position Yourself For Success.
    Get Out of Your Fantasy Mode. 53

Chapter 9
    Now Let's Make That Sales Call 57

Chapter 10
    Dealing With Price Objections 69

Chapter 11
    Win-Win Selling There's No Other Way. 81

Chapter 12
    Closing Techniques..85

Chapter 13
    Why Do You Keep Talking to the Wrong Prospects? 93

Chapter 14
    Relationships Trump Price, Every Time, Every Day, All Day Long. 107

Chapter 15
    STOP Selling Rice by the Grain! 113

Chapter 16
    Don't Under Estimate the Potential of Some Customers. 117

Chapter 17
    NEVER 'trash talk' Your Competitors. 119

    NEVER Interrupt a Sales Call..120

Chapter 18
    Life isn't fair... Better Get Used to it. 121

Chapter 19
    Start Learning About Your Competition........................125

Chapter 20
    Increase Your Odds of Success 100%
    by Getting Out of Bed..129

Chapter 21
    How to Destroy Your Territory
    in 3 Easy Steps 133

Chapter 22
    Purchasing People..137

Chapter 23
    Eating Crow..147

Chapter 24
    Get organized.
    Good grief, where's your customer list?.........................155

Chapter 25
    10 Habits to Stop Doing Now 159

Chapter 26
    10 Habits to Start Doing Now..163

Chapter 27
    A Slowing Economy...169

Chapter 28

Are You Working For The Right Company? Is your company dying a slow death? 173

Chapter 29

An Exceptional Opportunity 177

About The Author 181

REFERENCES..**183**

WHY I WROTE THIS BOOK

OVER 30 YEARS OF OUTSIDE SALES EXPERIENCE

When someone says they have 30 years of selling experience, you have to wonder, *how many of those years were going in the wrong direction? How many of those years were actually face-to-face with the customer?*

I've seen a lot of sales reps needlessly struggle with 'outside selling', because they don't understand what's keeping them from success. By ignoring the changes that purchasing people have made in the last few years they erroneously think that *things will eventually get better.* It is a difficult thing to face for even the most experienced professionals. There's a new mindset in purchasing taking place that you should no longer ignore.

It is much harder to get through the doors to see the actual buyers. Sales people don't have the *perceived value* they had in the past. Purchasing people have more knowledge and choices than ever before. The fact is, you are getting your clock cleaned by the competition because you aren't keeping up with the changes in your profession. It's time to take your selling experience to the *PRO LEVEL.* The one thing I have observed in the last few years is …the selling profession is rapidly changing and *there is a definite need to make some new adjustments.*

About 5 years ago I actually began to notice the shift. People in the purchasing world 'turned-on' to regularly using the internet as a tool. I believe it is in direct response to the fantastic e-commerce sites that these web merchants have developed, combined with their active social media presence. They are hitting the ball out of the park!

The way they are buying is changing, so the **the way we are selling needs to adjust.** They want things faster, cheaper and with bigger selections. You may say, "Larry that's no different than before, they have always wanted things faster and cheaper and with bigger selections." Right, but now they can actually get it, and you can't compete.

In addition, many manufacturers are adjusting to the growing pressures of competitive pricing and are now open to saying 'yes' to the customers that want to buy direct. The buyers can easily find them by searching on the internet. More and more transactions are going direct. The whole purchasing world just got bigger. Move over Mr. Sales Person, the buyers are no longer reluctant to embrace the web and all that it has to offer. E-commerce is soon going to take the bulk of the business.

This change was the inspiration for writing this book. How should sales people react to this internet explosion? Now that the **buying** has changed, your **selling approach needs to adjust**. That's what I set out to accomplish in these pages. Revealing the necessary changes needed to stay up with these purchasing trends. I believe what we are seeing in the market place, is **just the tip of the iceberg.**

ACKNOWLEDGEMENTS

I can actually attribute my big 'selling break' to a friend from my High School days, named Don Scardami. I knew him as a successful sales person early on, and he is the one that gave me the inspiration to try outside selling. He nudged me to fill out an application at the company he worked for. I have a lot to thank him for. Without that nudge, I know things would have gone very different for me. Thanks yer-buddy!

I was interviewed by the owner, Jeff Louis. I told him during the interview "Do not hire me if you have no intention of putting me in outside sales."

He is the second one I want to acknowledge, for this type of person is *rare* in our day and age. Jeff Louis was the single most inspiring mentor I have ever known. When I think of him... the word 'integrity' jumps out. He was a boss of purpose and opportunity. He was a leader, and a doer. I worked hard for him because I believed in him and believed in his vision. He was fair, honest and patient. He was never in 'over his head'. He knew what he was doing, and everyone knew it. I say 'Thank You' Jeff Louis for including me in your team. I will always be grateful for the opportunity you gave me. Thanks for taking a chance on me.

And now I want to give a big *Thank You* to Kevin Kingston. I appreciate your words of encouragement to write this book. You may not realize it, but you did have a great influence on my decision to just *'go for it'*.

SELLING AT THE PRO LEVEL

INTRODUCTION

A friend of mine asked me if I thought if sales people were becoming obsolete. "Isn't the internet taking over and pushing sales people to the curb"? It is true that there are many products that sales people no longer need to sell face-to-face. The products have changed, but the need is still there. Would you buy a solar power system without a sales person? How about doors and windows for your house? How would you get a chance to see new products that have been invented that might save your company a lot of money? Sales people will always be needed. Many companies rely on their sales people to assist them in finding the right product and getting it to them fast. Sales people are some of the most used and abused people on the planet. This is why many sales people simply cannot hang in there. **Fear** is a big problem.

Over 30 years of outside sales has *not* made me fearless. I still hate being rejected. The weary feeling comes when you approach a new prospect. It is something that you can't avoid, however you can learn from it, and process it in your mind so it doesn't affect you personally. I eventually learned to guard my mind and feelings. I learned to become resilient, just like an athlete that is determined to succeed. You press on by 'putting-off' your negative *self-talk* and 'put-on' the positive *success talk*. Don't allow yourself to wander off into the negative abyss. I am a product of motivational books from about age 19. The first book I read that changed the way I perceived everything was

"Think and Grow Rich" by Napoleon Hill. Written in 1937, this personal development and self-improvement book helped me to dream bigger dreams. It became the foundation of my 'thinking positive' brainy way of living. The second book I read that added to my mind explosion was "How To Win Friends and Influence People" by Dale Carnegie. It is amazing to think the impact these two books had on me at an early stage. This is just a confirmation of the fact that *we all need help* to have breakthroughs in our thinking that save us from the pain of the bad decisions we often make.

It's important to take responsibility for your bad habits and stop playing the victim. Why is the #1 salesperson doing so much better than everyone else? Fess-up to the fact that whatever you are presently doing is not working to the level you want it to.

Let's take a journey to see if you are doing some of the things I did over the years that I now consider, huge mistakes.

CHAPTER 1

FROM LOW LEVEL TO PRO LEVEL

The sales person of today must not appear to resemble anything of the sales people in the past. While you weren't looking, selling techniques and purchasing habits have changed dramatically. The ability to search for 'anything' on a computer has become a huge game changer.

When I was a little boy, my mother used to make flower arrangements with plastic artificial flowers. At the time, they looked so real to me. But over the years, my eyes became accustomed to them and I could no longer be fooled. Not even from a distance.

The same is true with salespeople. In the past, the difference between a plastic salesperson and an honest one was hard to figure out. They *all* seemed the same...plastic. Their closing techniques were so bad that I think people just bought things to get the salesperson off their back. Purchasing people have now become so accustomed to salespeople they can no longer be fooled.

Even the science fiction movies of the 70's looked 'cutting edge' back then. If you look at them now, you say "Wow, they look so phony , they are even hard to watch."

Perhaps one of the reasons you are struggling is because the game has changed, and you are just now figuring this out. Selling has definitely turned a corner, and the old way selling is now fading away. You may not like to hear this, but you cannot deny that everything in sales is quickly morphing into something new. Look at this recent statistic.

'Once at the heart of the US consumer experience, the ubiquitous mall is in crisis. Of 1,200 across the country, just 50% are expected to be in business by 2023'
theguardian.com/us-news/2017/jul/22/mall-of-america-minnesota-retail-anniversary

This is only to illustrate the fact that all segments of purchasing are changing, including retail. You have to ask yourself *"What is the future going to be like?"*

EXPECTATION OF SERVICE
The way you get your news is no longer through the newspaper. The way you watch a movie is no longer with a DVD. Even catching a taxi is now a new experience. Manufacturers are looking at their suppliers as problem-solving, information gathering resources, not a place just to order materials and hang up.

The *'way'* people want to buy things has changed. You cannot be the same old salesperson you have always been. There is an 'expectation of service' that companies are demanding. You need to be more than just their salesman. The term 'Lean Manufacturing' is where they want to go. They want less inventory on the shelves. They want you to ship what they want *only when they need it.*

Technology is dominating all industries. In some aspects, it is replacing the value of a typical salesperson. The 'average' salesperson is not going to be as successful anymore unless they pay attention to their environment. You are competing with other reps that are *exceptional* in your field. Right now, they are kicking your butt. You are also competing with the internet. Many purchasing people simply do not need a salesperson for a large portion of their purchases. Your 'brand and value' must stand out as *the best way to go*, when they do need help. Adapting to the new way of selling is where we are you are not in Kansas anymore. You need to get your selling skills to the *PRO LEVEL* as quickly as possible. I believe it is the only way a sales person can actually make the big money. The trend is to become a *trusted advisor* and a *partner* that knows their business and understands how to help them get what they want. You want to be considered a 'High Value Resource'. Your company has to be *forward thinking and continuously evolving*. Companies need to re-evaluate their 'go to market' approach driven by major changes in purchasing behaviors. Everything is moving towards web based, demand driven supply chains. The internet started on August 6, 1991. It took a good 10 years for people to figure out how to sell to the consumer. Then it became easier and easier to pay for things on the internet. The smart companies invested in e-commerce sites, and the whole world opened up to the purchasing sector in the manufacturing industry. You have to be aware that all this change has made a profound effect on the role of sales people. They have to fit in differently than in the past. They have to evolve and adjust to these new conditions.

Customers want to be able to depend on you and your company to support them. They expect you to have a keen understanding of your industry and keep up to date with emerging market trends. Innovation is on the move. Your customer will consider you valuable if you show interest in *their* company and *their* needs, in *their* industry, and even more valuable if you show them how to *save money* thru your company.

Studying your competition and understanding where they excel is of great value. Remember, they are also adjusting to the new trends and may have already left you in the dust. It may just be a matter of time before you realize, they have updated their website and are getting set up to *dominate your market*. I discuss this further in a chapter called 'Start Learning about Your Competition'.

It's time to 'up your game'. 'Relationship driven strategy' is still the key element to selling success, but it is quickly changing. Let me repeat that again, *it is quickly changing*. I discuss this further in the chapter on Relationships.

TECHNOLOGY MAKES US SMARTER

The salesperson of today has some major advantages over the past. We have huge amounts of analytic data at our disposal. You need to access it and use it like never before. There is so much information to gather on your customer that you are presently not even looking at. You can find out if they have stopped buying from you before you notice it on your paycheck. You can find accounts that have suddenly become explosive. Go and *secure* these accounts before your competition reads this book and finds them. Look at what they are buying. Ask them what their needs are? Buyers crave value. **Help them save money.** They will be forever bonded to you. Get that 'relationship' established.

As I began to write this book, I reviewed some of the books that I used to read over and over again, for inspiration and sales instruction. I was reading this one book and I couldn't believe my eyes. I partially closed it to look at the cover again. I wanted to know, was anyone endorsing this book? Yikes, it was one of my heroes. I had to look on the back to see what else was there. This was hard to understand. I looked at the copyright date, 1947. What, 1947? Good grief. This book is ancient. No wonder the methods seemed so out of date. They simply put a new cover on an old book and called it 'new' again. Now that's what I call *bad selling*. I feel sorry for the person in sales that's just getting started. They purchase a book like that and actually think the selling methods are sound. Wow, talk about a set-up for failure. Pay attention to the copyright dates of some of the books you read. Some of that old stuff will send you completely in the wrong direction of your success journey.

I picked up another of my old 'selling' books and I said to myself, 'I used to think that was good stuff'. I now consider it New Age and intellectually dishonest. So many of those principals were *dead wrong* and *did not work* or they just created more confusion. Even when I first came across some of those ideas that seemed hard to 'take in', I used to convince myself, 'it must be because I still don't get it yet'.

All these years later, I wonder if some of these writers actually believed their own stuff or were they just trying to sell more books. These characters were representing themselves as 'professionals'. I have always been skeptical of instruction. It comes from my rebellious attitude as a youth. Not all of their suggestions were off-base, but there are a lot of things that would get you thrown out of a prospects office if you tried them today.

NO PSYCHO BABBLE HERE

This book does not have any of that tricky psychological salestalk. I have set out to give you 'real world' wisdom from a guy that has *actually been in outside sales for over 30 years.* I have been 'in the trenches', not on the motivational talking circuit making millions of dollars selling books. I believe I have material that can actually make a difference in your selling career and turn you into a high-performance selling machine, if you have a hunger to learn. I dislike the cheap sounding sales people as much as anybody else. The one thing I want to get across is this, the *way* we now have to approach our customers' needs to be more *intelligent* than in the past. Customers don't want to waste time talking to a salesperson, so they are making it harder to get 'face-to-face' with them. Make your time count and pay attention to the *details* I lay out in this book.

This is not a business development book. This is specifically for the individual that wants to have a breakthrough in their selling career and is aware that sales people need to adjust their strategies to the changing trends. It is designed to get you to stop thinking like an amateur and start thinking like a Pro.

Chapter 2

The Results are In… And You Did Not Make The Top 10, Again

Success is No Accident

A customer once told me *"You are the only sales person that actually seems to be interested in what I do."* It made me feel good, but also made me think of the impact I had on this guy. I wondered if I repeated that same act of 'genuine interest' would I be able to achieve similar results? So I set out to become a better sales person by asking more questions about their business. Not only did it bond me to the customer, but it was actually fascinating to hear these entrepreneurs tell how they started their business from nothing. It taught me, that all they had was an 'idea' to start with, and they mixed it with hard work and the 'guts to take a risk'. The more I probed, the more I wanted to know. It made selling so much easier, but it has to be done over a long period of time. I learned to *take the focus off myself and put it on the customer.* It made me want to become an entrepreneur. I was always looking for a great side business that I could get into and someday turn into a successful business. I was on the hunt. I asked every customer that seemed friendly, and boy were they willing to talk.

Then came the recession, it went from bad to worse. My small customers were suffering badly. They were laying off great employees left and right. Many lost their houses and their businesses. Some customers even moved into their shops just to survive. These are the stories you never saw on the news.

In all of this, I was able to learn about being an entrepreneur during the 'easy times' and 'the toughest of times' without personally getting hurt. This was the best education about survival and success one could ever get. I have seen where they fail and I have seen how they grow from minnows to whales.

WHY SALESPEOPLE FAIL

There are certain types of people that seem to do great in the sales profession and then there are those that are a complete disaster. I have worked with some of the greatest salesman in the world and learned many reasons they are considered 'the best', I have also seen countless people 'try' selling and fall flat on their face. Here are some of the top reasons I think people fail at sales.

-No Desire or Vision -They just aren't motivated enough.

-No Desire or Vision -They just aren't motivated enough and don't believe in themselves.

-No Hustle in their Step – They think they can be successful the 'Lazy Man's Way' and never trying to get to the *PRO LEVEL*.

-They just don't Process Challenges without taking it personally- They let their emotions mess with their head.

-They don't keep their eye on the target. – Loosing focus.

-They don't communicate effectively at work to leverage ideas and strategies.

-They don't take advice from other successful sales professionals and in fact, they don't like any advice from anyone.

-They never read any current books or articles on the selling profession.

-They are still using 'old school' techniques.

-They aren't good problem solvers. –They lack creative solutions.

-They don't go into sales calls with a plan.

-They don't ask for the order. Their **fear of rejection** is so high they just keep selling & selling & selling until they lose the sale.

-They keep seeing the same 20-30 customers over and over again and fail to prospect for new ones.

Outside sales will give you an experience of living you cannot find in any other profession. You will have your hand on the 'pulse of life' outside the office cubicle. You will witness the hard work it takes to survive and the rewards to those that take the risks. You will feel 'alive' and inspired with your surroundings. You will be able to look at the mountains and watch the rain as you drive around town. Feel the sun on your face. You will be free to express yourself and free to think and dream. If you are a salesperson that has to travel a lot, you will have plenty of opportunity to educate yourself while on the road. This is like a gift to a person that wants more in life. If you get an education in many areas, you will always be given more opportunities. Learn about selling, and you will reap the rewards of 'Selling like a PRO'.

WHAT IS THE SILVER BULLET?
You may say 'But Larry, I'm not there yet." "What am I doing wrong?" "I'm not near where I want to be." "Why am I struggling?" *"What is the Silver Bullet?"*

You want the answers 'now'. What 'is' the answer? How do you get more sales? Where do you find more customers?

Whenever the Olympics come around, I always ask myself 'What drives these people to reach this level of accomplishment?' 'What is motivating them?', 'What would happen if I put as much focus, drive and energy into my job as they did?' I know I would be unstoppable!

The answer is 'desire and action'. You have to want something so bad you are 'willing do whatever it takes' to achieve it. Desire is the fuel that propels you to go beyond 'average'. Action is what it takes to get there. Your problem might be found in 'what you are *NOT* willing to do' to achieve the success you desire. Hello? Are you still there? You know exactly what I am talking about. *The successful sales people are not copying you. Why is that?*

Your 'desire' has to push you to find out what you are missing. I hope this book is your start. You need to make a 'decision' to be great, just like an Olympic athlete. You will never become great by accident. You are going to have to 'dream' of what you *could* become. No one is going to do that for you. Dream big, get inspired. Make this your year of explosive growth. A firecracker will not go off by itself. It has a lot of 'explosive power' inside but nothing will happen until it gets a spark. The same is with you. There is a lot of untapped potential in you… it just takes that spark. Let us not fool ourselves *you are going to have to be uncomfortable.* There I said it, *you are going to have to be uncomfortable*, Ha, just said it again. Don't worry, the feelings will go away and you will be left with a great income and an awesome future. Don't talk yourself out of a great income in sales because you are afraid to put in a little 'extra effort'. Every great achiever that makes it to the PRO LEVEL in anything does so because they put in that extra effort. You can't be great at anything without getting past the 'average' attempt to succeed.

The enemy to your success is *the comfort zone* you are swimming in.

In fact, I saw you doing the back-stroke at work the other day. Turn your body 'over' we are going to a new pool. Your competitor is already there.

> *"Successful people do the things that unsuccessful people are unwilling to do."*
>
> *— John C. Maxwell*

SELLING AT THE PRO LEVEL

"The quality of a person's life is in direct proportion to their commitment to excellence, regardless of their chosen field of endeavor."

— Vince Lombardi (Considered by many, to be the greatest football coach of all time.)

Chapter 3

Listening to a Mentor

Johnny had no skills for anything else, except cleaning toilets and washing dishes. He was terrible at both, so he decided to go into sales.

Selling is one of those professions that most people start with absolutely no experience or training. It is a profession that *requires you* to have mastered some basic communication skills and to have a good understanding of the psychology of people to achieve any success. It's no wonder most people that try sales just can't hang in there. It would be like a rookie baseball player getting into a game with major league professionals. You aren't going to have a good experience.

A recent survey revealed, a whopping 55% of sales reps don't have the right skills to be successful. (the Brevet Group)
www.thebrevetgroup.com/21-mind-blowing-sales-stats

Professional players of all sports spend years perfecting their craft, yet most people that go into the sales profession think they can 'learn as they go'. It is true you don't need any special degree to get into sales, just guts. Well that was me. I had no experience. It could have been such a disaster, luckily I made it through. To 'stay' in sales you need wisdom… the more, the better. Lack of wisdom will eventually bite you so hard you will be thinking the job cleaning toilets is a good back-up plan. Don't leave your selling success to chance.

MAKING SMALL SUBTLE ADJUSTMENTS

Professional athletes master the basics and then spend the rest of their career making small subtle adjustments that take them to astounding levels of success. They are constantly listening to a mentor or coach for their whole career.

They don't take critical suggestions personally. They want to be encouraged. They want to be directed. They want to be successful, and will try anything that could get them there. Does that sound like you? Don't cheat yourself of potential breakthroughs because you don't like to take advice. Listen to the top people in your field. Keep getting knowledge from mentors, seminars and books and you will find yourself breaking out to new levels of achievement. It will also carry you through some tough dry spells. Get a winning attitude. You need to be determined and fearless. You can do great things if you dream bigger dreams and stay focused.

It's the small adjustments that you should focus on. You might be doing something that's bothering your potential customers.

You keep doing it over and over again. By making a few subtle changes you could find yourself in new levels of personal success.

Perhaps one of the reasons you are struggling is because you don't know the problems you are creating for yourself.

Selling is the best job on earth when you understand the psychology and timing of it. You can't do this alone. It will cost you too many years to gain enough experience to make a good living doing it. Take a short-cut by reading how others have turned bad decisions into 'life-changing lessons' of profit. Many of the most successful people have also had some of the greatest failures. That's the gold you want to dig into.

THAT LITTLE EXTRA

"The difference between ordinary and extraordinary is that little extra." — Jimmy Johnson, Head coach, Dallas Cowboys (1989-93), Miami Dolphins (1996-99)

That 'little extra' can be the difference between an average income and a *great* income. 'That little extra' is something you might get out of this book that can give you the breakthrough you've been looking for. Pay attention to what you are *not* doing. What do you think you are doing that *isn't* working? Could it be prospecting, or the way you are treating your customer? Maybe you need to structure your customer visits differently. Are you really giving them the impression you care about them? Are you following up on your promises? Are you getting lazy in your approach to selling? Are you asking for the order? Are you contacting them enough? Look on the floor... did you drop 'the ball' somewhere?

A good example of what I am talking about is when you go out to a restaurant, and your waitress is *something special*. She is genuine, personable and just very good. She actually makes the whole meal taste better. You feel obligated to give her a nice tip. Why? *Because that 'little extra' she gave you is not normal out there.* It really stands-out when you experience it. What could you do that would stand-out to your customers? What is the 'little extra' you can do in your territory?

GET PERSPECTIVE... HERE

When I started, I felt unstoppable. Everything was going my way. It was a huge learning curve, but I was up for the task. As time passed, I started to notice resistance from customers and began to doubt myself. It was getting harder and harder to make progress. I kept pushing and pushing. I expressed the challenges to my company and they gave me a motivational talk that went something like this *"Just hang in there and you'll be ok."*

You will doubt yourself in selling. It comes with the job. You are not alone. Selling is a hard job. It becomes a 'battle of the mind' at times. But let me tell you something, *it is in no-way so difficult you cannot make it through.* The challenges you will face in selling, don't come close to the challenges others are facing in this world, and they are living victorious, productive lives.

There is this guy named Nick Vujicic. He was born with no arms or legs! It is called tetra-amelia. I have had the privilege to see him speak on two occasions. This guy is the most amazing human being that has ever lived. Go to You Tube and hear him speak. He does his speaking on top of a table. You will be forever changed.

In his autobiography he says his mother was so afraid, she refused to hold him at birth. She had the nurse hold him in front of her. Eventually she accepted his condition and learned to love him like a mother should. This guy has it rough. Despite all of the obstacles you can think of, he struggled and came to terms with his condition by putting his faith in God and pressing on. He founded an international organization and ministry in 2005 called <u>Life Without Limbs</u>

He met a beautiful woman named Kane and married her in 2007. They now have two boys and more on the way. This guy is the bomb. He gives hope to all those that think they have it tough. He inspires and encourages people as a living. He is a living testimony to the importance of faith, perspective and humility. Just think how easy it would be in his condition, to just check out and say I'm never going to amount to anything. While he does admit it was difficult growing up, he faced his challenges and rose up to tremendous greatness rarely seen in any person of today. Keep your head on straight, you've actually got it easy.

Nothing is easy to the unwilling.

Wishful Thinking

There is so much *positive mental attitude* talk that often borders on 'new age' psychology. I am greatly opposed to the notion that you can tap into some mental power and manipulate your life by simply 'believing'. The philosophy suggests you can manifest things to happen in your life by 'believing' in them with purpose and intensity. There was a famous guru that often said "I will see it, when I believe it." Well that's an interesting saying, but it is far from true.

If you are 5'-9" tall, you cannot 'believe' yourself into growing 7 inches to becoming 6'-4" tall. No amount of 'believing' can make you stretch your body like that. Yes I do believe it is of great value to have a *positive mental attitude*. It is all over this book. But it needs to be **realistic**. What I am talking about is 'disciplining' our minds to avoid the traps of negative thinking. Let me give you an example.

Let's say you are driving on the road and rushed to get to an appointment. You hit a red light. You hit another red light. And now you say to yourself "If I hit one more red light I'm going to scream." Your anger does not reveal anything about the red lights, it reveals *something about you*. You see, red lights are good. They keep us safe and keep order and progress in society. They protect us from on-coming vehicles etc. But your *attitude* about red lights is the real problem. If that negative input goes unchecked, you will eventually become dangerous to everyone around you. This is how some people end up becoming manic depressants. They *allow themselves* to focus on something negative for so long, if it goes unchecked, it becomes who they are and how they perceive reality.

We all need perspective and help when we find ourselves in a rut. Is our anger warranted? Is our anger way out of perspective? Are we dealing with reality here?

Another example is a salesperson that believes they are not ever going to reach the $1 million dollar goal. That may be wrongful thinking. The question they need to ask themselves is, "*If it were possible*, what would I have to do to achieve it?"

Believe in yourself 'YES'. Believe in unrealistic goals, 'NO'

Believe you can get yourself out of a *negative* rut, YES. I've seen it and done it thousands of times.

Believing and visualizing you can putt a ball onto a hole 20 yards away, YES.

Believing you can find 3 new customers in one month, YES.

Believing you can go one month without being late to an appointment, YES.

Believing you are good enough to earn that spiff, YES.

Believing you can grow your sales by 25% in one year, YES.

Believing you can see one more customer per day, YES.

That is what gives us so much hope. Focus on the possible. Stay away from the negative impossible.

The Desperate Salesman

Selling is a serious business. Don't try to be a jokester sales person. It's great to have a sense of humor in your style, but if you are just getting to know your prospect, stay away from the jokes. I've never known a 'Jokester' salesman to be in the top of his field. Jokes are not always funny to everyone. You are taking the risk of creating unnecessary objections to you and your company. It's so easy to say a joke that will offend someone. Most jokes that are being passed around today are about politics or sexual in nature. What you say about sexual preferences, politics, race or religion can destroy a business relationship so fast it will make your head spin. Price will not matter if your customer is turned off by your character. You want your prospect to trust you, so reduce your potential for resistance by acting as professional as possible. Elevate your game to include the policy of not telling offensive jokes *of any kind*. That means there will be very few you can repeat. You want to be known as a professional sales person, not a part-time comedian. Perhaps you have been guilty of doing this and are still unaware that the reason a customer may not be giving you any business might be because of something you said in the past that actually offended them.

> "A man must be big enough to admit his mistakes, smart enough to profit from them, and strong enough to correct them."
>
> – John C. Maxwell

CHAPTER 4

PERCEPTION IS HUGE.

Your biggest problem may not be obvious to you, but boy is it obvious to everyone else.

Bob had been talking for about 5 minutes and the person he was talking to finally said "you have something on your teeth". The whole conversation was being interrupted because the person listening could not stand another minute looking at the stuff on his teeth.

What if you have something about you that the listener cannot possibly tell you?

Things like, your perfume/cologne smells horrible? How about the shirt you are wearing has a food stain on your chest. Your long fingernails are grossing them out. Your clothes style is just wrong for sales. Your breath is worse than a camel's rear. These can be barriers before you even get started.

First Impressions Matter

Alexander Todorov is a professor of psychology at Princeton University. He recently wrote a book titled Face Value: The Irresistible Influence of First Impressions. (2017) Considered to be cutting-edge research, he discovered that we make up our minds about others after seeing their faces for only a fraction of a second (.1) by flashing a photo of someone on a screen. He then asked the viewer to give their impression of the person in the photo. Given even a longer period of time to see the photo, it did not change the mind of the viewer. It does not actually reveal anything about the person in the photo, but it does expose something about us. How many times have you had the wrong impression about someone when you first met them? The first impression a prospect has of you, is very important.

There is a level of competency you need to achieve to survive in sales. People expect you to 'fit the part'. The Best salespeople always look the part. It's perfectly ok to have an unusual personality type as I believe most successful sales people have. It sets you apart and often times can be your greatest asset.

You need to develop credibility from the moment they meet you. Their perception of you is everything, so let's not make it any harder than it already is. To them, perception is reality until they get to know you.

Your personal hygiene must be top notch.

A Deal Breaker

This is not optional. It will be a 'deal breaker' if you have anything about you that stands out as weird, gross, sloppy or annoying. You must not give your potential customer any reason to show resistance to spending time with you.

-Too much cologne.

-Bad breath.

-A strange hair-cut.

-Teeth that are off-color.

-Clothes that are wrinkled.

-Clothes that are out of style.

-Shoes that are worn out.

-A wrist watch that looks cheap.

-A cheap looking pen.

-Dirty hair.

-Too much jewelry.

-Over dressing.

-Under dressing.

-Clothes that don't match.

-An offensive tattoo.

If given a choice, your customer will prefer to do business with an average looking 'professional' than someone that is drawing attention. Am I suggesting 'dress for success?' Yes. Get serious about your image.

You have to sell yourself, before you can sell anything to your customer.

I learned an interesting thing by accident when I changed jobs. My new employer provided custom embroidered dress shirts to wear daily. The logo design was beautiful and made me feel official and professional. Much to my surprise, accounts that at one time did not let me see the purchasing person, ushered me in with no resistance at all. Time and time again it was as if the embroidered logo said 'Police'. Many times when I was out somewhere for lunch, strangers would come up to me and ask questions about my company. An embroidered logo shirt immediately screams 'professional company'. If your company is the type that can justify a custom logo shirt, get it done... you will be pleasantly surprised. Look the part. It will make your job easier and well worth the investment.

Selling Like A PRO

I have a friend that is a top seller in his company. He stands out as one of the best there is. He happens to have tattoos all down one arm to his wrist and always wore a long sleeve shirt to cover them. One day I caught him at lunch and noticed he had on a short sleeve shirt. I made the comment that "times had changed so much in the last few years that he no longer has to cover up his tattoos". He said "I have a long sleeve shirt I put on when I am meeting new customers". He said "I don't want to start off with the wrong impression." Wow! That is exactly why he is a top seller. He realizes that image is so important that he is not willing to risk creating resistance on a new prospect, until he establishes a connection first. He knew it could be a distraction to the initial meeting.

Now that's selling like a PRO. That's exactly what I mean when I say, "You need to sell yourself first!"

Business Cards

Do not hand out business cards that are bent, dirty or wrinkled. Your business cards should be professionally designed. These cards are often times the only thing your potential customer has to judge the quality of your company.

If your card looks hokey,

your company is hokey.

Therefore, you are hokey.

And your dog should be named 'hokey'.

Image is *EVERYTHING* in the sales profession. Don't talk yourself into believing your cards aren't that bad. Yes, they are bad, nasty bad! Image is 'everything' in every profession. *Pay attention to the details.* Good grief, get a nice looking business card!

Brand Yourself Now

Odds are you haven't put much thought into how you can be different from your competition. If you don't differentiate yourself from everyone else, you become a commodity sales person, and are stuck with the *'low price'* war. You are no different than the next guy. You need to *become different.* What do I mean by that? You have to have a value-added reason for calling them. Letting your customers know that you are *unique* in the market place. It's called 'branding'. The bigger the company the more visible the branding becomes. Why is that? Large companies understand the value of branding and the importance of their image. They want to control how they are perceived in the marketplace. Most of these companies started with a good product or idea, and then started branding themselves to take their offering to the *next level*. They invest lots of money to carve out a *brand* that is going to make them look exciting. The results are astounding. The Starbucks branding is a good example. It's not just the coffee that's great... it's everything else, the logo, the atmosphere, the food items, their uniforms, their attention to the customer. There is an *expectation* of service or quality when you deal with these companies. Starbucks is very focused on how they are perceived. They are always changing the look of their interior to give you the impression there is a lot of new things going on. They don't want you to get comfortable with the same old signage. They want it to look fresh every time you walk in. They are the *leader* in the coffee industry because they are the trail blazers of marketing and branding.

You want to position yourself with a company that is concerned about how they are perceived. Why not work for the best company in your industry? The best run companies are always looking for the best reps. They want the top notch people to represent them, and are willing to pay a higher price for them. They don't just hire them based on a terrific resume. They do background checks to explore their reputation out in the industry. I have been contacted at least a dozen times by various companies over the years, asking about an individual and their reputation. These were not reference checks, these were 'exploratory inquiries', off-the-record discussions. Before hiring a 'high dollar' individual, they want to know what they are buying.

Yes it is important that the company you work for 'brands' itself, but it is equally important that you create your own 'brand' or style of selling. This is what separates you from the other guy. It is the 'experience' that your customer feels when they do business with you. Do they *feel* like they are working with the best guy in the industry? People buy emotionally and they are always worried about their feelings. You want them to *experience* what professionalism is like. Your competition may have a better selection, *but they don't have you*. You are the difference. You return their phone calls quickly. You respond to their requests for quotes more promptly. You are easy to get hold of. You keep them up to date on the latest new products. You actively show them how to save money at your company. You are dependable, courteous and all about 'taking care of business'. They want you on their team. You can be the reason they don't price shop. You can keep the competition out by proving to your customer you are hungry for their business and are willing to climb the highest mountain for them. You can obligate them to give you a try. Act fearless. Be sincere. Stand out as the salesperson that is going somewhere with his/her life. It's contagious. They will want you around. You don't have to fear the competition if you never give your customers a 'reason to leave'. Better yet, if you give your customer a 'reason to stay', *they'll never leave you.*

BRAND YOUR COMPANY NOW

You have to know what makes your company special. You literally have to tell your customer how to think about your company. If you don't do this, your competitor will 'brand' you, *and you won't like what they have to say*. Don't exaggerate, but don't hold back either. There are things that can stand out if you look for them.

The obvious areas we should look at are:

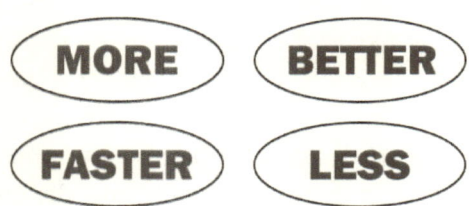

More

- More selection
- More options
- More inventory
- More choices
- More value

Faster

- Faster lead times
- Faster response times
- Faster delivery
- Faster quotes
- Faster turn around

Less

- Less hassle
- Less minimums
- Less paperwork

Better

- Better selection
- Better hours
- Better educated team
- Better delivery
- Better terms
- Better services
- Better salespeople
- Better quality
- Better paperwork
- Better looking
- Better system
- Better people
- Better value
- Better attitude

NOTICE: *Pricing was not on any of the lists.* Why?

Lower pricing always means lower profits. Don't forget, you are here to make a profit. Try not to rely on pricing only. Your company is also selling value and service, and it costs a little more.

What you're really after is *loyalty* to your brand and *loyalty* to your company brand.

You want your customers *hooked on the way you do business.*

So how do you get your branding message out there?

First off, something has to look different about your company. Maybe your logo, your tag line or your business cards could be upgraded. You could get new embroidered shirts to wear. Your customers need to *see* some change. Many large companies change their logo every few years. Why, because they want to force their customers to see that something has changed about the company. They want to put to rest the old image and *bring on the new.* When was the last time your company made an image change? As a sales person you need to also make an image change. Throw away that old shirt you've been wearing for two years and go and get some new clothes. Look at your shoes, they look tired like you.

HOW DOES YOUR ORDER DESK ANSWER THE PHONE?

The way the order desk answers the phone can change slightly. "Thank you for calling Smith Manufacturing, how can we help you?" They need to *hear* some change.

Does your company have vehicles that have your logo and new tag line updated on them?

Do you have a nice looking footer under your email signature? Is your company logo there?

Thank You.

Johnny Smith

12345 Second Avenue Suite #37
Los Angeles, California 90000
(213) 228-8000   x 111
jsmith@advancesm.com
advancesm.com

How about distributing a new flyer about your company that has a fresh look about it?

How about 'Telling them' about the change that is happening? Are you open for business earlier? Can you offer same-day delivery? "But Larry, what if my company has no changes to talk about?" Good grief, can't you make something up? You need to become the 'change'. Do I have to come up with *everything?*

Start 'becoming' the type of sales person you think would make you stand-out as the best in your field.

There is a huge supplier that most manufacturers know about. *They are always the most expensive!* They never sell on price. They sell on service and availability only. That is their 'brand'. They always have what you want 'in stock' and they can get it to you *faster than anyone else*. This proves that price isn't the only thing of value to the customer. This should be a good lesson to all suppliers out there.

30-50% Of Sales Go To The Vendor That Responds First!

thebrevetgroup.com/21-mind-blowing-sales-stats

This has been true throughout my career. I can't tell you how many times a customer said that my competition failed to get back to them on a quote request. If you make a commitment to follow-up with your prospects in a timely manner, you have won half the battle. Even if you don't have an answer, it is very important to call them and say "Thanks for your patience, we are still working on it." Your main goal is to out-perform the competition. You will only get a few chances to do this. If you do it often enough, you can win the customer over and reap the rewards of passing the test. It actually makes the competition look bad when you are outperforming them.

Give your customers that 'little extra'. Get serious about giving them 'knock your socks off service' when you can.

Chapter 5

A Selling Technique That Will 'Blow Away' Your Customers

Bob was a go-getter. He tells his prospective customers that his company 'blows away the competition on everything'!

What that actually means:

Bob is saying, that his company is so advanced, that they have developed ways of doing business that no other company has ever seen or understood. They have mastered it to such a level that 'everything' is better than the competition and thus you are getting hosed when you buy from your present supplier.

The worst selling technique you can use is 'over dramatizing' things. Using too much emphasis with your words is called 'over-selling'. This is a sign of an inexperienced sales person. When I say this technique will blow away your customers, I mean they will leave.

"Climb aboard, this here is the best looking car on the lot, and it is a steal at this price."

"Our customers 'rave' about our good prices every day."

"Our Solar Panels are 1000 times better than the competition"

"Our window units blow-away everything you can find out there, that's why they're so expensive."

"For once in your life, you have found the best tires for the price."

"Our awesome kayaks are indestructible and make everything out there look like a cheap kid's toy."

  This is why sales people have trouble selling. Unprofessional 'sales talk' immediately puts up a red flag.

Don't Ever Dramatize
Make a commitment to say the truth *even if it is not so good*. You will develop integrity with a customer that will serve you well. It will put your customer at ease with you.

"We do a good job servicing our customers. We don't always get it right, but we fix it and strive to do better"

"Our Blackstar tires aren't the best tires you can buy, but they are a great value at this price."

"Because our window units would be considered a 'premium product' on the market, they command the higher price."

What a difference. It brings integrity to the presentation. You diffuse the argument before they can even bring it up. Pay attention to the way you have been talking, are you guilty of over-selling?

You Need Wisdom

I always make it a point to have audio sales training material in my car. There were many times I was stuck in traffic, so I would listen to something like The Secrets of Negotiating by Roger Dawson or Tom Hopkins material instead of talk radio or music. It's the best way to get an education while you are working.

It is true that you don't need a degree to go into sales. You just need 'courage' to stay in sales. You also need *wisdom*, - lots of it. You are responsible for your education and success. You need to get serious about your career. You need to become a professional. Fix what is in your power to fix.

Do professional athletes ever stop training... *absolutely not!* In fact they train even more when they're getting paid for what they do. If a team makes it to the Super Bowl, they don't relax weeks before the game because they think they have finally arrived and can now take a break. Professionals of all types are keeping their skills at their top level by getting advice and working to get better. Sales reps often begin to relax when they start to make some decent money. How do I know that? Because that was me! Just when I thought I deserved a break and began to think I was unstoppable, I lost a great account. A PRO is always aware that the competition is right behind them trying to get that account. The wheels can come off the cart at any time. Stay at the top of your game at keep learning about your profession and your customers.

Who are the greatest sales training professionals of all time? What are the greatest selling 'sales' books of today?

CHANGED FROM THE INSIDE OUT

Get on Amazon or Google and start consuming loads of wisdom about your occupation. There is so much good stuff out there, hundreds of books on every aspect of selling. You will be changed from the inside out. It will forever make you a better person and sales professional. One book can motivate you for life. Start reading today. There are lots of 'sales' videos on You Tube that you can watch for free. **Learn to 'earn' your living.** I have a large collection of motivational books at my bedside. I mark in them with pencil as I am reading them. That way I can easily find the gold nugget next time I pick it up. You need to believe in yourself.

Part of your problem is you are filled with self-doubt. You may ask, "Well how can I believe in myself if everything I have done up to this point in my life has been a disaster?"

-You need to be convinced of your potential.

-You need to have a desire to get better.

-Envision yourself having a 'breakthrough' that is life changing.

-You need to be self-confident and motivated.

You will really begin to love the profession of selling when you start to figure out how to get better at it. Do it with integrity. Become a PRO. I will be first to admit that selling is not always easy, *but it is not always hard either*.

> *"If it is easy, then you are doing it wrong."* -- Gabby Williams, guard, UConn basketball team.

Be the expert in the field you sell in. Customers feel comfortable with someone that has more knowledge than they do on a subject. Learn and memorize certain details about your product or service that would impress even an average listener. This is how you develop *credibility*... the gold-standard in sales.

> *"Confidence comes from being prepared."*
>
> -John Wooden

SELLING AT THE PRO LEVEL

Chapter 6

I'm sorry Mr. Customer, What was Your Name Again?

If you don't use your customers' name, they will most certainly notice it!

You've been talking and talking, trying to establish credibility, and your customer notices you are not using their name in your small talk. This is big. I know a salesman friend that called everyone 'boss' because he was too lazy to figure out a method to remember his customers' names. He never reached the level of Top Salesman amongst his peers, and I believe this was the biggest reason. One day I did a ride-along with him and it struck me as odd that he called everyone 'boss' and he told me that people actually 'like it'. I think he was delusional. It was ridiculously uncomfortable when he tried to introduce me to his customers.

I Have it All in My Head

I knew another salesman that never wrote down any of the names of his customers because he said he had it 'all in his head'. I don't care if you are Albert Einstein; you cannot possibly keep up with all the changes out in the field. Even Albert Einstein had to write everything down.

First off, the single most important thing a customer likes to hear from a sales person, is **his own name**. Don't ever forget that. It shows tremendous respect to the individual. It shows that you consider him so important, you have remembered his name. When you don't remember his name, it says 'You are just another customer in my day. Not special and not very important to me.'

Get Everyone's Name You Can

I have always made it a habit to **know as many names as I possibly can**. Get interested in everybody at a company. This has been one of the greatest keys to my personal success.

-It keeps the competition out.

-It builds impenetrable relationships.

-It makes it much easier to do business.

When an employee leaves from a customer, they often called me to their new job to see if I can do business with them. It is a valuable tool, and I want you to understand the importance of this. Do not try to 'wing it' when it comes to your customers' names. You have to get it on an Excel List. You have to be able to get *instant access* to the information. I have tried so many ways of doing it. I'm certain you could put it all in your phone on some kind of app, but I came to the conclusion this worked best for me.

Create a spread sheet in Excel.

-You want a column for the Account Name.

-A Column for the City

-A large Column for Contacts

-A Column for Phone Numbers

This will eventually be printed out in landscape format. When you type in the Account Name, keep it condensed as much as possible. You are going to need all your room for the Contacts column.

Starting with the first person you come in contact with at each account, start listing their names. For Example: Connie-Receptionist,

Connie–Rec., Bob-Whs., Mgr., Sandy- Purchasing, Tom- Pres.

There Are Changes Every Week To Be Made

As you work in your territory, you will discover there will be changes to the list every week. This is why, if you had it on your phone, there would need to be a lot of editing that I prefer to do at my office. For example: Sandy was promoted to accounting, Connie quit etc. Jeff is new in the shop. You make a note on your sheet. Handwrite the new names etc. My list usually consisted of about 5 pages of customers. After about 3 months, it was time to update the list in Excel.

The reasons I put the list in Excel are the following:

You pull up to an account and you want to ***instantly*** get the name of the receptionist before you go in.

The sheet is organized by city, so it is easy to find the customer. You also take a look at all the other names that might be there. Now you are equipped to say 'hello' to Connie and Bob and Sandy when you walk in, as if you were great friends. Remember, '*Boss*' is not a persons' name.

▪ What ever method you decide to use, I am convinced you will never make it to the PRO Level if you don't have a method to remember your customer's names. If this does not sound like good advice, you will be struggling for years and your competition will clean your clock. Imagine you are in front of your customer and you don't remember his name. He says he wants to order one of your products. You ask him if he wants to use a P.O. number on the order and he says "Sure, just use my name." You are looking like a fool. You had better pick up a business card as you walk out.

CHAPTER 7

WHY AM I DOING THIS ANYWAY? THERE'S GOT TO BE AN EASIER WAY TO MAKE A LIVING...RIGHT?

There has never been a greater time to be in sales than right now. Why do I say that? You have information and technology at your fingertips like never before. You have accumulated history about an account that can be accessed in seconds. Most companies have analytics about your customers that is so valuable. You can find out who has stopped buying in the last month, or who is slowing down their purchasing? Which accounts are fast-growing? You have mobile phone technology that carries more information than any time in history. You have GPS to keep you from wasting time looking for an account. You have years of accumulated knowledge about the profession of selling. This is your time. This is your chance. You have it all! You just need to grab it.

THERE IS A REASON

There is a reason that two people can buy the identical tomato plant, and plant them. One person produces volumes of large tomatoes, while the other one simply cannot.

There is a reason my wife can iron a shirt and it looks 10 times better than when I iron the same shirt, with the same iron.

There is a reason that two people can have the exact same ingredients for a cake, the identical oven, and one of them does not come out as well as the other.

There is a reason two doctors can see the same patient, and both of them have a different diagnosis as to the same problem.

There is a reason two sales people can have similar territories and one is a major success, and the other is barely hanging on.

There is a reason that one sales person can sell a product at a higher price, while another one can *never* sell at the higher price.

THE ANSWER IS

I have seen these things over and over again. The answer is a simple one. A closer examination of the problem always reveals the missing link. It usually boils down to *education*.

There is an adjustment that needs to be made somewhere. Sometimes just a 'small' change can produce 'big' results. That's exactly what I hope you can get out of this book. Examine yourself to see if there needs to be a change. You need to study the reason you aren't getting the breakthrough in the area you want victory. Ask another sales person to guide you. Find out 'exactly' what they are doing differently than you. It's called 'modeling', model after them. Do exactly what they do. It may not be as exciting as you would think, but they are doing some things that you aren't, and they are making a big difference in their sales numbers. You are not penalized for trying. Use some of the tips I have put in this book. You **can** have success, if you commit to it.

"Never let the fear of striking out get in your way."

-- Babe Ruth, seven-time World Series champion.

I want you to be successful at selling. I want you to have a breakout year. I want you to experience the excitement of helping entrepreneurs be successful. Not everyone has rhythm and timing to be a professional dancer or a voice that could sell music, but 'selling' is something almost anyone can do if they believe in themselves and believe in their products. Selling is a learned skill that can be perfected over time. If you have a teachable spirit, you can shorten the learning curve and end up making a great living in a fantastic profession.

"The difference between a successful person and others is not a lack of strength, not a lack of knowledge, but rather in a lack of will."

-Vince Lombardi

When I said *'there is a reason* my wife can iron a shirt and it looks 10 times better than when I iron the same shirt, with the same iron.' I was serious. I wondered what was the reason?

Well, I asked her and she said something I didn't expect. She said *"It's because I love to iron."* I never thought anyone would love to iron. So that made me think, maybe that's the key to getting better at some of the areas we struggle in. We need to learn to love what we are doing, even if it seems strange. If you changed your attitude about some of your struggles, you definitely would be a better person and sales person.

Chapter 8

Position yourself for success.
Get out of your fantasy mode.

I know you think someday soon you are going to land a huge account. You keep thinking... all I need is 3 huge accounts and I will be OK. So you get the courage to see a few prospects. After each visit you tell yourself 'that was a good stop. I think I impressed the purchasing person. She seemed to like my story about how bad our competitors are. I think they will be calling me soon.'

They never call. Why? I told them we were the cheapest in town and we outperform all our competitors in every way. All they need to do is call me and I will 'blow their mind' with the best prices they have ever seen! Why wouldn't you respond to that? I wasn't obnoxious in any way. **What's wrong with them?**

First off... they were on to you when you walked in the door. They knew in advance that you were going to be like every other sales person that strolls in. They had no intention of switching their supplier to you. *They weren't even looking for a new supplier.* After all, they have been doing business with your competitor for over 20 years. They have a great relationship with Bob their sales rep. and they are very happy with the level of service they get. It's no wonder you hate the large accounts.

Second... How did you get into that large account? They rarely allow sales people like you to stroll in like that. Congratulations, at least you got past the gate-keeper. She must have been a new receptionist.

92% of salespeople give up after no sales on the 4th call. 60% of customers say no four times before saying yes.

nugrowth.com/wp-content/uploads/2015/03/NuGrowth_SalesStats_0315

When and if you get in front of an actual buyer, you will get only ONE opportunity to make your presentation. You need to use all your sales psychology know-how to get this right. You want to been seen as the 'High Quality You', a real professional.

Third...Have your professional looking business card ready. Do not start looking for it once you get in front of your buyer. Do not pull the bent dirty one out of your wallet.

Thank them for their time. Hand them a professionally made brochure that covers the basics of your company.

You might mention the product lines you specialize in. Then casually mention that you know they have good established suppliers and you just want to be considered a **'Back-up'** source for them. (A 'Back-up' source is reasonable and non-threatening.) Mention you'd be glad to help them if they ever need your services. Get one of their business cards. **Now get out.** They are already getting tired of you.

All companies need 'Back-up' plans when their existing suppliers drop-the-ball. Every supplier, no matter how good they are, will eventually drop-the-ball. This is usually your only chance to start the process of building a relationship. ***Relationships are what you are striving for***. Don't ever forget that. Relationships are the foundation to your success. A short e-mail 30 days later would be acceptable. Don't be a desperate sales pest.

SET ATTAINABLE GOALS

You might want to say I want to find one new account per month that has the potential to be in my top 20 list. That becomes the *one thing* that is always on your mind. It keeps you focused on 'achieving' rather than focused on the obstacles or distractions of daily activities. Keeping your eye on the target is a habit of all successful athletes and all great achievers.

Every day I create a list of things ***I plan on accomplishing*** for that day. I have done this for over 30 years. It is a habit that has proven to be very successful. This is a proven habit of all PRO Sales people. You want to keep the 'pressure on' out in your territory. Make yourself visible. Visibility is important to establishing credibility and long term commitment. Visibility keeps your possibilities open.

Create goals that set you on fire.

If you want more from life, you can't wait around for everyone around you to get their act together. Top Sales Pros blaze their own trail! You can't wait for management or for a pie-in-the-sky promise from a customer. You can't ride the coat tails of someone else's dream. You have to get your own dreams. You may say, "Larry, I don't have any big dreams." Oh boy, you are a sick puppy. Don't come to me with that bad attitude. You go and find your dream, *and you do it now!* You sit your butt down and start pretending you hit the lottery. Without a dream, you are halfway in the grave. You might as well be a wax statue. No dreams, no goals, no fire. No way.

I want you to be successful at selling. I want you to have a breakout year. I want you to experience the excitement of helping entrepreneurs be successful. Not everyone has rhythm and timing to be a professional dancer or a voice that could sell music, but 'selling' is something almost anyone can do if they believe in themselves and believe in their products. Selling is a learned skill that can be perfected over time. If you have a teachable spirit, you can shorten the learning curve and end up making a great living in a fantastic profession.

"You will always miss 100 percent of the shots you don't take."

- Wayne Gretzky, Canadian hockey player and leading scorer in NHL history.

CHAPTER 9

NOW LET'S MAKE THAT SALES CALL

If you weren't getting paid to do this, I don't think you would ever do it voluntarily. The reason salespeople command a higher income, is because there's a price for all the pain and suffering they have to endure.

You've been putting off seeing this prospect for some time now. You pull your car over to a shady spot near a curb. Now you are one street away from the company. You just want to sit and think for a minute. "I want this account, but I know it's going to be difficult to get." In your mind, something is taking place. The air becomes thick, fear is showing up. You look thru your notes, pushing papers around on the passenger seat, fidgeting and stalling. You imagine in your mind, how you want to approach the building, how you are going to ask to see the purchasing person, how you will react to the receptionist saying 'Tim is not available". You look in the mirror, hmmm my hair is kind of out-of-place today. You check your phone, no messages. You look at the time, 9:00 AM and say to yourself, maybe this is not the best time to see a new account. Checking your customer list you find an old account that rarely buys, Jim is a friendly guy. You start your car and say to yourself "I'm just going come back after lunch." As you drive past the building, you are so relieved. Sadly, fear has won again. The reason I can write this, is because it has happened to me many times.

FEAR

Fear is a protection mechanism in your brain. It's what keeps us from getting hurt, but it can also keep us from *being successful*. It hinders achievement. It shows up in selling, on a daily basis. It interferes in your pricing structure. It messes with sound logical thinking. It can become your enemy. We need to learn to recognize it, adjust for it and get some victory here.

Fear keeps us from getting hurt, but it also can keep us from being successful.

With all the experience I have had in front of customers face-to-face, you would think I should have mastered the 'fear factor'. Well let me tell you, it's no different than a person that handles cobra snakes. By keeping a small amount of *'healthy fear'* in your brain, it will keep you from slipping into the stupidity mode. The reason you see extreme sports people get terribly injured, is because they turn off all notion of fear and pay a high price for it.

When a person has a terrible fear of something like 'bugs' for instance, a talented coach can help them overcome the fear by 'confronting it' in a safe way. Little by little the fear is diminished until it is in line with reality. This has proven to be the best way to deal with this *'unhealthy fear.'* Little by little I have learned that my fears were not warranted.

So let's look at confronting the fears you are having at a sales call. We will start with the fear of seeing a new account, or an account that you might have not seen in a very long time or a cold-call prospect.

THE PLAN - WHEN SEEING A NEW ACCOUNT

You have to ask yourself the only question that really matters, 'What is the worst thing that could happen?' That's it. Once we get thru this exercise, you will see there is actually nothing to fear (but fear itself).

If she asks, "Do you have an appointment?" Just say, "No thanks, I'm just barging in without one."

Yeah right. The one thing I deal with in my mind is the thought that I feel like *an intruder*. I know I am on someone else's turf. I am entering on their property without prior notice. I do not suggest to, *stop cold-calling*. In fact, cold-calling is a big percent of my success formula. Yikes! I know what you are thinking, I want to be successful in sales, but I want to do it **without** cold-calling. Good luck. That's like saying, I want to be a doctor, but I don't want to see any blood. I want to be a professional surfer, but I don't want to be in any cold water. I want to be a professional football player, but I don't want to have any pain. I want to be great, but I don't want to be uncomfortable *in any way*. The highest paid people on this earth are actually getting paid big money, because *they are doing what you won't do!* You have to stop thinking like an amateur and get out of your cushy comfort zone. The reason cold-calling is effective is because many customers are also in a comfort zone, and will never *discover you* on their own. So you need to *discover them*. Let me mention at this stage, if you are selling swimming pools, or real estate or insurance, cold calling may not work for you. I am talking about industries where cold-calling would be an effective approach.

Here are some of the worst things that could happen on an 'unannounced' sales call. You walk up to the receptionist and ask *"Can I talk to the person in charge of purchasing?"*

-"I'm sorry you will need to make an appointment first."

-"Jim is in a meeting at this time, can I take a message?"

-"Thanks for stopping by, but we don't need anything today."

-"No thanks, we're not interested."

-"We already have enough suppliers."

-"We are happy with our present supplier."

-"We don't like your company."

"We are good for now."

-"Let me see if I can catch him."

-"Sure, go right on in. That's his desk."

-"That would be Bob he is in the room on the left."

See anything earth shattering? No. So... what's the problem? The bug you are afraid of is just an ant! It won't kill you. Repeatedly confronting your fears will eventually give you resilience and strength. Now you might say something like, "Oh that's fine, I would like to know the best way to get in touch with your purchasing department." Or "What is the ***proper way*** to contact your purchasing department?" Or "When is the best time to catch him?" Be polite, you may not get what you want, but in my experience, if you look professional you often times will get a name or an email. Sometimes if you disarm the receptionist it can be a great door-opener, say "**Hello, I'm not here to see anyone,** *I would just like to know, what is the proper procedure to contact the purchasing person?*" Many times this has given me an escort to the right person *on the spot.*

Salespeople actually fear 'rejection'. Nobody likes to be rejected. It is something you cannot get used to. As a professional, you learn to mentally separate yourself from the process. It is not *you* they are rejecting, it is the fact they don't want to be 'challenged' themselves. Your timing may be part of the problem. It seems like there is never a *good time* to be interrupted. Keep their response in perspective. I have been amazed to find many customers will actually give you a chance to talk.

SALESPEOPLE AREN'T LOVED

Many people do not like sales people. This is because they have never met you, right? It is true, if they don't know you, they immediately judge you as a sneaky, pushy sales person. After all you don't have to go to school to learn how to sell *and it shows.* You only have seconds to prove them wrong. Your first impression has to be your best. If you get your chance to see a purchasing person face-to-face, ease into your introduction, upbeat, confident, interested and smooth. Like someone who is wealthy and confident, but not puffed-up. Make your planned presentation… discuss how you might be able to help them. Ask if they are the decision maker? Ask them if they have heard of your company or done business with your company in the past? Ask them if they might consider you as a source in the future? Ask what process they normally go through when considering a new vendor?

Find out if they have anything they are presently looking for that you might be able to help them with, and then get out! (Remember you are a busy sales person and have lots of other appointments. You are not desperate for a new client.) Do not stay too long on your first visit unless it is warranted.

I once saw a survey that said;

The #1 thing purchasing people hate about sales people is... they talk too much!

DON'T BE A WASTE OF THEIR TIME

This was one of my first mistakes in sales. I had no idea they had no time for me. After all, I had products they actually bought on a regular basis. You would think they want to know all my knowledge and pricing for things, right? I used to challenge them to tell me the price they are presently paying for something. This is the worst selling technique you could ever use. No one ever taught me this technique. I learned it all by myself.

You are not there to entertain them. They don't know you and they don't want to know you. They are interested in their friends. Just look at their Facebook page. They have over 500 followers! They post everything about their personal lives as if they are movie stars. They think everyone wants a piece of their fame, fortune and time. They have hundreds of selfies posted.

Happy smiles, as if their life is amazing and they have so many friends. Life is so good. They even show you all the food they eat. Look, here I am in Hawaii. Oh, here I am at the beach. That's me at the Taylor Swift concert. Our seats were so close to the stage.

You are nothing. You are just a sales person. *Just leave your lousy flyer and head to the big door over there.*

Sorry, it's true. Have a nice day. This is why salespeople have 'fear'.

> *Only 13% of customers believe a salesperson can understand their needs.*
>
> *thebrevetgroup.com /21-mind-blowing-sales-stats*

In other words, 87% do NOT believe a salesperson can understand their needs. You should think about that. Customers should be convinced that, you *understand what they need*. Asking more questions about the specifics of what they need is the way to overcome this.

The Plan - When Seeing an Existing Account

PRO Selling always requires a plan. You cannot just 'drop in' to say "hello". How successful would a professional tennis player be, if they went out on the court without a strategy? They most likely would get slaughtered. Many sales people have no strategy. That is a big mistake. You need to have a *good reason* to see your customer or you have no business going there. Don't just go to your customer to *visit*. They have a business to run and you have a job to do. Perhaps that is the single biggest reason you are not reaching your goals. (Oops, you have no goals?)

Don't ever go into a sales call without a plan

OK so how do we make a plan? I'm glad you asked. First off, let's just admit your 'winging it strategy' is not as successful as you would like. Let's also admit, you have not been selling with the thought of 'exceptionalism' or 'purpose' on your mind. This is why you are experiencing 'fear'. Now that we have exposed the problem, we can move on to the cure.

Action is a cure for the fear. What kind of action? Prepare yourself. Preparation is the key answer. You already knew this. Interesting how we already know the answers to most of our daily problems. The challenge is we fail to act on our own wisdom.

Ask yourself,

'What do I want to find out during this call?' or

'What do I want to accomplish here?' or

"What is a good reason to go visit this customer?"

Setting some type of goal is a good start. Do you have all the sales literature or brochures, or samples you need to make the presentation? Do you have the paperwork with you if the customer wants to place an order on the spot?

METHOD OF DISCOVERY

PRO selling should not be a sneaky trick to get someone to buy. It is however, *a method of discovery* to find out what your customer really wants and needs. Finding out the challenges they are currently facing and then listening. They will let you know if there is an opportunity or not for you to pursue. Over the years I learned from many sales trainers, you need to be asking the *right* questions.

The one who is asking the questions is always in control. You will never sell anything to anyone that they aren't already looking for. But if you think you can just talk and talk and talk and eventually get a sale, maybe you should try selling ear plugs in the middle of your presentation. You'll sell lots of them.

If your lips are flapping, you are not learning about what your customer wants. The longer you talk without stopping, the sooner you will be escorted out the door. You need to find out **who they buy from** and **why** and **do they need what you have to offer?** If you don't know this information at the beginning of your contact, you are destined to waste time. You need to make sure you are dealing with the decision maker.

You need to maximize your potential for success. This is valuable information you simply can't do without. Do you think a franchise goes into a territory without fully and carefully understanding what they are up against? You cannot 'wing-it' here. Chapter 19 (Start learning about your competition.) is going to help you. Don't measure your success by how much 'product knowledge' you have. Your biggest success will be found in learning about the sales profession and 'branding your selling style'. Selling is a psychological and strategic game. It requires more knowledge than you presently know. All the knowledge about selling could not fit into a 1,000 books. It's sad that most sales people start with no training. Talk about a set up for failure. That's like parachute jumping without training. Good luck.

How about asking questions that have meat on them? Like...

"Mr. Customer, if it was possible, what would it take to earn some of your business?"

If he says "It's not possible." Then you just saved yourself a lot of wasted time and got a reality check on a long-term unrealistic pipe dream. See, you're already getting smarter.

THE PSYCHOLOGY OF SELLING

Why do people buy? What is the most important thing a consumer or purchasing person is looking for? Every sales training book has something on this subject. According to a recent study by UPS called, UPS Industrial Buying Dynamics Study, they interviewed 1500 industrial buyers across the U.S. and rated **product quality** at the top of the list when it comes to distributor performance. **Product availability** came in second. Everyone is expecting a quality product. *Availability* is the game changer. Purchasing people have pressure to get things fast. If your company cannot perform at break-neck speed in this day and age, you might not be able to capture the customers that you want.

The word 'SALE' is a testimony as to the power of wording. You put that word on some products and it somehow triggers a switch in the brain of some consumers that defies logic. I don't believe however, everything should be on sale all the time. In fact too much of it begins to diminish the quality of your company and brand.

All of these examples are proven to work on the buyers emotions. It makes them *feel good* when they see them. People want to *feel* like they are getting a break. They want to think they are making a *good buying decision*. This will often push them into the buying decision. Honey, I saved us $100 today...that's great babe, how'd you do it? These $300 shoes were on sale!

If you see an ad for car tires that says, "Buy 3 get 1 FREE", consumers so badly *want to believe* they are actually getting one tire for free, they will beat their brain into submission to justify it. This is mental gymnastics and marketers know how to play on the consumers weak emotional triggers. Trust me...you are not getting a $50-150 tire for free. You are actually paying for it. There is enough profit put into the price of the tires to justify 'giving one for free'. No company can stay in business by giving away product. If it sounds too good to be true, it is. To prove my point, you will never hear of a gold coin company say, "Buy 3 gold ounce coins at spot price of $1200 each and get one free." Sorry to burst your bubble. Everyone needs to make a profit or you will be gone in no time flat.

With that in mind, your customer wants to believe *so badly* what you promise, that they will defy normal logic to get it. You might say "We have the best selection at the lowest prices and no backorders," they actually want to believe you, even though they know it is impossible to do. It makes them 'feel' good. Like somehow your company has been able to do what no other company has been able to do. If you cannot perform on your promise, you have proven to be just like all the others. This is why you need to 'brand' yourself as a *straight shooter*. The guy who tells it like it is. This kind of salesperson is rare, but it's where you want to be.

Selling would be great if you just didn't have to deal with customers.

Making More Money with Less Customers

If the 'Cost-to-Serve' your small customers' is no longer profitable... it is time to raise your prices. Does this sound too aggressive, not at all. Getting rid of the non-profit customer *transaction* is the best business decision you can make. I'm not saying kick them to the curb. I am saying *raising the minimums to make it worth it*. The small customers often use a lot of resources from your company and they are the first to complain. Often times, they are getting a better deal than they deserve. Every company has small customers, and every company needs them to keep the inventory turning. A small customer can turn into a very valuable medium customer, so handle them with the mind-set that they will eventually be worth it.

For additional commentary see Chapter 25, on page 159. **Stop Seeing High-Maintenance Low-Profit Accounts**

Chapter 10

Dealing With Price Objections

Customer:

I like your company, but your price is too high.

What he actually means is:

I like your company, but your price is too high.

There are times when you cannot get around it. You'd like to focus on the 'value and service' to offset and justify your higher price, but when you are selling the **exact same product** for **more money** than the competition, you've got a real problem on your hand. There is always someone willing to sell a product at cost, or near cost. Why, you may ask? I have asked that question my whole career. It just doesn't make sense. Why leave so much on the table? Why not make a profit? That's what you are here for, right? The only explanation that makes any sense is... **they don't know their actual landed costs.** You feel like calling them and saying "Hey, let me help you figure out the basic 'Cost to Serve' math. You guys are losing lots of money." There's also a philosophy that says "Don't argue with profit, no matter how little it is." Good grief, is this what they are teaching at Harvard Business School?

If you are a manufacturer a product, you might be able to cut costs in some areas. Eventually there is a number you can't go below and most likely, you are already there.

Selling by 'volume' is a reasonable justification to have a low gross profit and *it is the only one that makes any sense.*

Importing is also a game changer. If you are up against a guy that is importing the same product, your chances of coming close to him are 'slim to none'. He also has room in the price to go even lower if he has to.

A note of caution;

When your customer says 'your price is high' be sensitive to the fact that your prospect may not be giving you the whole truth. He may not be mentioning the terms and conditions that are associated with his pricing. He may not mention that freight is not included or that there are contingencies attached to the price. He may not mention that the price was a 'one time deal'. Not that you want to think he might be playing you, but it does happen more than I want to say.

PRICE IS NOT ALWAYS THE ISSUE

It seems like price is ALWAYS the issue but the professional trainers say otherwise. They kept saying "Price is **rarely** the issue." I used to think they are only using that logic to justify using 'sales psycho-babble closing techniques'. I struggled with this a lot. The only thing I could conclude is… they don't know what they are talking about. I have never had a customer say, *"I want to pay a higher price, if that is possible."* My reasoning went as follows: If you give me the lowest price product, I will be writing orders *all day long*. It seems like the only thing everyone cares about anymore is the cheapest price. Prove to me in a logical, intellectual way that price is **not** the issue. Go ahead, blow my mind.

Well guess what? I started thinking about this and discovered I am wrong in many instances. When I want to have a hamburger, I go to The Burger Lounge. Why? It has nothing to do with price. It's the quality I'm after. They serve the 'worlds-best' grass fed beef burgers. I could care less about the price at this point. I actually don't even know how much their hamburgers cost. If price were the only issue, I would most likely go to McDonalds.

The same is true when I buy shoes. I'm not interested in the 'cheapest' pair of work shoes I can find. I'm looking for nice shoes, at a 'reasonable' price.

The same is true when I get dental work. I don't want the 'cheapest' dentist I can find, I want one that does good work at fair market prices.

The same is true when I go out to breakfast. I go to a place that has nice service and good food. I do not like to wait a long time for my coffee to be refilled. Price is not the determining factor here.

The same is true when my customer said "We come to you because your competitor *Discount Dan's*, screws up every order we give them."

The same is true when a customer says "You guys always have what we need 'in stock'. They never mentioned price.

The same is true when a customer says "We are buying from you because **we feel** you actually know what you are talking about". This is an emotional decision, not price.

The same is true when a customer says "We heard our competitor is using you, and thought we should give you a try."

The same is true when a customer says "Our neighbor down the street, bought one of your solar power systems and they seemed very happy."

The same is true when I want to buy coffee or paper plates or toilet paper, **the cheapest will not do**. It's not about the price.

How about when you buy sunglasses? Do you look for the cheapest?

I now believe buying the 'cheapest' is actually rare at my house. I don't want the cheapest carpet in my home…or the cheapest paint on my walls, or the cheapest bath towels I can get. I don't want the cheapest bed I can find or the cheapest couch to sit on. "Hi honey, I'm home! Here, I bought you the *cheapest* flowers I could find."

Get my point? Stop making **price** the only feature you have! I believe it becomes the 'only issue' when you treat it as *'the only issue'*.

There is tremendous 'value' in *quality or quick turn-around. Customer service* is a huge selling feature. It starts with the sales person. You have to be able to 'sell your customer service' advantage. You can ask your customer **"Is price the only factor you consider?"** He will say *"No, I also need quality and short lead times too."* Say

"Great, we have the fair price, the quality, and lead times you are looking for."

PRICE SENSITIVE PRODUCTS

If your product or service is 'Price Sensitive' and the exact same product or service at a higher price *you cannot play the price game*. You lose. You cannot sell $5 dollar bills for $5.75 when your competition is selling them for $4.85 'Volume' does not make up for the difference on this one.

I did not want to have to tell you this. But you are only left with the option of, comparing the *difference* between your company and everyone else. Not a bad option, if your company has great benefits, like daily delivery, order on-line, bigger selection of other products, terms, etc. You are also going to have to sell *yourself* as a 'benefit'. After all, you are the best rep out there, aren't you?

Let me tell you something about sales. Some companies sell strictly on price, "The low price leaders!" and some don't. I already mentioned this company when I talked about 'branding'. Mc Master Carr is the single best run supplier in the nation. Nobody comes *close* to their selection, depth of inventory and quick delivery. No one even comes close to them. Guess what? They **never** sell on price! They are always the highest price! Then why do people buy from them? Because, they sell on service, selection and delivery. They refuse to play the 'price game', **because they know you can't make any money by being the cheapest.** The lesson here is people are willing to pay a lot more, for extraordinary service and selection.

ARE YOU GIVING IT AWAY FOR FREE?

Maybe your company is already offering *extraordinary service and selection,* but you are giving it away for free. You aren't using it as a unique feature of your company because it's the 'norm' around there.

86% of customers will pay more for a better customer experience. https://www.groovehq.com/support/customer-service-statistics

67% said they would be willing to pay more money to get same-day delivery.
http://www.supplychainquarterly.com/news/20161004-survey-online-shopper--demand-visibility-as-well-as-speed-in-delivery/

44% said Fast Delivery would motivate them to give repeat business.
http://www.supplychainquarterly.com/news/20161004-survey-online-shopper--demand-visibility-as-well-as-speed-in-delivery/

The pace of change continues to accelerate. Consumers are willing to pay for speed of delivery. Statistics show, **consumers**

will often take increased delivery speed even if they don't need it.

Listen, you just can't offer both the lowest price and the fastest delivery, and make any money. It rarely happens, but somehow your company thinks they are going to be able to offer both *all the time*. This is not the norm for profitable businesses. Only Amazon can pull that off.

-Maybe your company can offer faster service ***for a cost***.

-Maybe your company can offer 'combo' deals. If they combine their order with other products you can justify a discount on the whole order.

-Maybe your company needs to raise the minimum requirement, for free truck deliveries as a way of offsetting all the lower pricing.

If you are selling commodity items, you will always have to play the 'low price game'. Don't complain if you are just like your competition and they are giving product away for 'little or no profit'. Specialize in the niche areas where there are fewer competitors. The bottom line is... *you have to make a profit* to keep this boat afloat.

PRICE VERSES COST

This is a great way to rationalize with your customer, why the product you sell is worth the higher price.

"Joe, our cobalt drill bit does have a higher *price* point, but the *cost* of each hole drilled, is dramatically reduced because of the longer life and faster drilling time."

The customer needs to be convinced the higher price is actually a good investment overall.

"Can You Beat Their Price?"

A customer may ask you *"Can you beat their price"*. Never say "yes". That just keeps the 'price war' game going. Get out of that pattern by saying this, "I'm not sure if I can beat the price, **but if I can, will you give me the order?"** If they respond with a "maybe", then don't quote them. Never give out your lowest prices without a commitment to buy! Often times they will use your numbers against you and force the other supplier to come down in price. This tactic, by the way, is a good example of *bad purchasing ethics.* This is the type of customer that I *rarely* go back to see. I make them come to me, and I never budge on price from that point forward. I know they are only calling me because they can't get it anywhere else.

Never Show All Your Cards

If they say "How is your price compared to Joeys Discount Parts Company?"

Never say, "We are about the same."

Say, "I don't know, what are you paying?, Does that include ___? How is their service, lead times, terms, etc.?"

Get all the objectionable information out on the table. You will then know what you are actually dealing with.

For Sale: A Non-profit-able business

According to a report published by Global Entrepreneurship 2015/2016 by Babson College;

Over 50% of businesses discontinue operations because of **lack of profits** *or financial funding.*

babson.edu/news-events/babson-news/Pages/1-19-12globalgem

Another study published in 2014 by the Turnaround Management Society reveals;

54.6% of business crises are caused by the mistakes of top management. The most prominent causes of a crisis are that **the management continued with a strategy that was no longer working for the company. They lost touch with the market and their customers and did not want to adapt to changes occurring around them.**

Why do Companies fail? 2014 Survey Results, Turnaround Management Society, 14 February 2014

Think about Radio Shack, Blockbuster Video, Sears, Sports Authority, American Apparel, and Thomas Brothers Maps. If your company fails to keep up with the changes in the market place, they have to cover too much ground to catch up, once they realize they are in trouble. The results of losing touch with your customers' buying patterns can lead to the eventual death of your company.

The Bureau of Labor Statistics, Business Employment Dynamics says, **around 50% of all businesses no longer exist after 5 years. Only one-third make it past their 10th anniversary.**

Businesses must either generate profit, or cut costs to survive. They need to generate adequate cash flow to meet expenses. As a sales person, you need to be mindful of making sure the orders you are taking generate enough profit to justify the processing labor. No-profit or low-profit orders can slow a company down to a screeching halt.

FEAR OF CHANGE

Customer:

"Bob, thank you for coming by, we know you have a good company, but we have been working with the same rep at Pestco Discount Products for so many years, we have no reason to change at this time."

What he actually means is:

"Bob, I like your company, but we are so set in our ways. We like to believe we can trust our present supplier & sales rep. We really don't want to know if he is taking us to the cleaners."

What you wish he would say is:

"Bob, I like your company, and I know you are a good sales rep. trying to make an honest living. How about giving me a price on your contact cement just to see how we are doing with our present supplier. Does that sound fair?"

Change is painful. It actually boils down to more work for the buyer and the possibility of upsetting his relationship with his present supplier. As I mentioned in a previous chapter, 'relationships trump everything'. At the present time, he has no relationship with you. He has no interest in changing anything. You have two choices, you can say, "Thanks for your time, great talking to you, here's my card, I'll be there when you need me," give a hand shake, then leave. Or your second choice is to start a relationship right there on the spot. The ultimate goal is to create 'leverage'.

CREATING LEVERAGE

What does that mean? You are going to plan on seeing him on several strategic intervals in order to get a relationship going. You want him to keep you *on his mind* when he finds himself in a bind. This will begin to put pressure on the customer to eventually give you something to quote. You will be showing him a new product or flyer on each visit. It will start like this:

"Jim I understand you have a great relationship with Pestco Discount Products and I wouldn't expect you to change what has been working so well over the years. I respect the loyalty you have to your suppliers. I was just wondering if you wouldn't mind if I stopped by the next time I'm in the area to show you a new product line I think would be of interest to you, I promise I won't be a waste of your time"

Or this one;

"Jim I understand you have a great relationship with Pestco Discount Products and I wouldn't expect you to change what has been working so well over the years. I respect the loyalty you have to your suppliers. I was just wondering if you wouldn't mind considering me as a 'back-up' source in the future."

Nice and short. If he says "no thanks" say "Thanks for your time, great talking to you, here's my card, I'll be there when you need me," give a hand shake, then leave.

You only have so many hours in the day, and you have to decide which customers have the *greatest potential for growth* in your territory. Be picky. Don't settle for prospects that treat you like you are a waste of their time. You can't get them all. You don't want them all. Getting to the PRO Level means you have to get strategic about your approach to making more money. If you are smart about your approach, you will definitely find open doors when you least expected. I don't give up on customers that I really want. Some accounts take a long time to break. I've worked on some accounts for years. Did it pay off? Absolutely! My best 'money making' accounts were the toughest ones to get into. The competition will hold on tight to those accounts. You need to be relentless and wait for your opportunity to prove yourself. You need to be there when they are in trouble. Never ever give up on an account that you know is a gold mine for profit.

Chapter 11

Win–Win Selling
There's No other way.

Jeff presented his product line like a professional. Everything seemed to be going good. Then his prospect leaned over to him and said, "Jeff, I like what you have to offer, but your prices are way too high. We've been paying half that from your competition."

What that actually means:

"Jeff, I like what you have to offer, but I've never pay the first price a salesman has to offer. I know from experience, you salesmen have plenty of room in your back pocket for negotiating."

The Desperate Salesman

You should never enter a sale without it being a good exchange for both parties. Only a fool would think he can get the better end of a sale, and expect a supplier to be ok with losing money. Never do business with a person like that. I have seen this time and time again. If a prospect is not interested in a win-win deal, move on to a better quality human being. You want loyal customers to your brand of company, your brand of selling, and your brand of service. The best customers are devoted customers, and there are many out there. It takes time to find your collection of good customers, but I can assure they want a loyal salesperson as well. A good salesperson, that can help them get the right products, at the right time, and they will be happy to pay a fair price.

89% of consumers have stopped doing business with a company after experiencing poor customer service.

slideshare.net/Right Now/2011-customer-experience-impact-report

When a customer has to struggle to do business with your company, they will go elsewhere. Often times you need to be the mediator between your company and your customer. Companies never admit they are difficult to work with. There are so many company policies that you would think they hate their customers. Every company I worked for has had issues with how they deal with their customers. Especially when it comes to returns. Expect this will be the same for you. Do your best to represent both the customer and your employer. You need both of them.

Save Your Customer Money

If you have a customer that is buying 'a pinch of salt' every day, help him to save money by giving him a bulk price for buying once every two weeks. The 'cost-to-serve' a customer that is constantly buying the same stuff over and over again, is bigger than you think. There is too much 'human expense' in processing a small order. I'm talking about;

-The labor entering the order.

-Packing the order.

-The financial transaction of the order.

-Delivering or shipping the order.

All this labor can be greatly reduced by giving him incentive to bulk up. At the same time, your company is making more profit. This is Win-Win selling.

SLOW PAYING CUSTOMERS

If a customer is slow-paying it is not a win-win. You cannot afford to give a customer *great pricing* and *quick delivery* and then have them not pay you on time. This is just bad business. Many customers will treat your company like it is a bank, *if you let them*. You essentially are financing their business venture. If they treat you like a bank, you in-turn should act like a bank, and slap them with those finance charges. I have had to pass on great opportunities with some fantastic companies because they have bad credit references. It doesn't matter how great the potential is, if they are going to put your money at risk by delaying payment beyond the signed agreement, you need to put them on 'hold' fast.

An important principal in business is to 'reduce your potential for loss.' If a customer owes you a lot of money and they find themselves in *financial trouble*, guess what? You are now in *financial trouble*. As a salesperson, it is difficult to accept the fact that you cannot do business with the fastest growing and largest company in your territory because they are slow pay. Over the years I have had to pass on some whoppers. I'm sorry to say, I was relieved that my company cut them off, after I heard they eventually went bankrupt. The losses some of my competitors had to take were staggering. The fact is, you never know how bad their situation is. They will not tell you they are being sued or they 'under bid' a large job or the competition has them on COD. Resist the temptation to ask your company to 'give them a chance'. Even in booming times, many customers go broke.

Don't waste your time going to visit them. These are business decisions you must honor if you are going to be a PRO. You are looking for win-win partners only.

There is a saying 'Don't argue with profit'. I agree, but what good is a little profit, if your customer takes 60 days or more to pay you? It seems hard to accept, but these accounts need to go to your competitor. If they go bust, you not only have to recover the small profit, but you also have to recover the landed cost of the product. That means you might have to sell 3 times more product just to break even. Yikes! Talk about going the wrong direction.

Chapter 12

Closing Techniques

You may say "I don't use closing techniques." yes you do! Most likely, you call them something else, like 'Helping the customer to understand the advantages of our service.' Or 'Finding out what is the most important feature they are looking for' or 'asking for the order.'

'Do closing techniques actually work?' Yes they work, but not every time. 'Closing' is a term used that means you are 'finalizing the sale'. It suggests that you are *handling all the objections* that the customer can think of, and then eventually leading them to the words *"Yes, I'll take it"*. You are essentially *disarming the resistance* of going ahead with the purchase. Is this a sneaky tactic? Not at all, if the method is done ethically, and you are honestly not trying to manipulate the mind of your customer, you are actually speeding up the decision making process. Helping your customer answer all the questions they might have about your product or service is a sound practice. The closing techniques are a way of *fishing out* any objection that might appear at the end of the decision to buy or not to buy.

It is no different than you persuading your son or daughter that they must finish school and graduate. You start by asking good questions to find out their reasoning of wanting to quit, and honestly answer them one by one until they have no more viable objections. Is that considered sneaky? No, it's considered love.

Simple Selling

Some sales professionals say "You should be using closing techniques *the minute you walk in the door."* If you have regular customers, don't try this. You are revealing your in-experience. Not all selling requires a closing technique. Some customers just place an order and it's just a matter of processing the paperwork. Other customers require a special price or a delivery deadline. Sometimes all it takes is *showing up* and you get the order!

> *"The world is run by those who show up"*
>
> -Unknown

I have found that customers like a salesperson that keeps in touch. They are not put off by my visits. In fact, they begin to *expect I will drop by* and prepare an order before I get there. Some have a list prepared of the things they want to talk about. Be active and visible in your territory. I can go for months and never run into my competition. I often ask myself "Am I the only guy out here selling?"

Closing techniques are used to help the customer 'reason through' objections that might be an issue to them. Helping them get over the *fear* of making a wrong or bad decision. Things like, "Will this product do what you say it will do?" "Are you giving me the best possible price?" "Can I make small payments over 6 months?" "What if I find out it's not working for me?" all lead up to the buying decision.

SUBTLE CLOSING TECHNIQUES

Closing techniques should be so natural sounding that your customer would never know they are being used.

Customer: "Can I have it tomorrow?"

Salesperson: "I don't know if I can get it to you tomorrow, but if I can, *will you take it?*"

Salesperson:

Is there anything else you might need to know?

Is price your only concern?

Would you like to go ahead and take it?

How are we doing?

Are you ready to take one?

EMOTIONAL WARFARE

It is always a lively discussion when I discuss with my colleagues the ethics of some closing techniques. Every one of us has, at one time or another, bought something we didn't want, or wish we would have not bought at all. Somehow we got caught up in the *emotion* of the moment. We came home with that blender we actually never wanted. Well guess what? That is exactly what marketing and selling is about. Getting the customer *emotionally* involved in the purchase. Most *all* of marketing is an *emotional* sell. There has been so much research on 'why people buy' that marketing organizations have mastered the art of manipulating the buying experience. If you study it, you will feel vulnerable because you will quickly realize, you can be easily convinced to buy almost anything, *emotionally*.

People are afraid of salespeople. It is justified especially when you understand how easy it is to sway some people. Not everyone can be manipulated all the time, but everyone is being manipulated at some time.

> *Most marketing is just an emotional sell.*

The reason salespeople have such a challenge, is because customers know they are vulnerable to a smooth talking professional salesperson. They don't want to be challenged with their reasoning skills, because they are not prepared to defend their position. They know there are *tricks* and *techniques* that can be used on them. It's all true. Do they work? Yes, especially with inexperienced buyers. This is why I have a hard time with some industries that completely take advantage of willing victims. They get in the 'combat mode' and become determined to do whatever it takes to close the sale.

Many customers know in advance, they are going to be pressured to buy, even if they don't have the income to pay for it. Look at the housing bubble for example. Many of these homes were sold to people that simply could not afford them.

Closing is a learned skill. It must be honest and ethical.

PUPPY-DOG CLOSE

Research has found, the more *emotion* you can get into your presentation, the better. Showing your product is one thing, but handing it to your customer is best, or letting them try it. This is why auto salespeople always want you to test drive any car. They know, if they get you behind the wheel, statistics show, that you will fall in-love with the car, just like you do when you are handed a puppy dog. The odds of the sale go off the charts!

Get your customer emotionally involved in your product by having samples they can *touch* or letting them *smell* the product. If you are selling a food product, the customer can hardly resist if they can *taste* it first. Even if it is a wood sample let them *feel* the finish. All these things help tremendously to lowering the resistance of a customer. This is exactly why people buy things they never knew they wanted. This is also why advertising is always letting you know how you will *'feel'* after you purchase their product. Clothing ads always show people so happy in their new outfit. Truck ads always show how manly it is to own their vehicle. You are being sold *emotionally* all day long and don't even realize it.

MATCHING YOUR BUYERS STYLE

Some good advice I've heard on closing the sale is to match your buyers' style. Don't try to outsmart them with your product knowledge. Fall in line. Most selling is understanding what your customer wants and *how they want to buy it*. Be smart about how you handle people. It is more important as a salesperson than any other profession. Being flexible in your selling approach is the only way that will work.

Most selling is, understanding what your customer wants and how they want to buy it.

If your buyer is calm and laid-back, you should become calm and laid-back. If your customer is a jerk... *don't become a jerk*. Keep your head on straight and let him make a fool of himself, without your help. It's all about 'people skills'. Learning to handle all different types of difficult people will make you an absolute success in selling and also open doors to opportunities you never expected. If anything, selling will give you a priceless experience of the people and world around you.

Sometimes a customer has a specific routine every time they will purchase from you. They want to haggle first, and then they give you an order. If you take offense to their buying style, maybe PRO Selling is not for you. If you understand that this is their style, and you can make a profit at it, this is a win-win. You are on your way to a great career.

Disruptive Close

This is a 'drop a bomb' on your customer technique. The idea is to break the positive mental picture they have about a particular brand.

You ask the customer "What type of silicone spray lubricant are you using on those bearings?" They say "We use brand X."

Then you say "Oh, that stuff, did you know that it is highly flammable?" meaning that it is very dangerous. Then you present them with your Non-flam product. You may not always have a product that has an advantage over the competition, but if you do, drop the bomb.

THE ALTERNATIVE CLOSE

The Alternative Close is over used and obvious if not used correctly. The idea is to give your customer two choices, both answers are a win for you and moving you closer to the final sale.

"Would you like it in white or blue?"

"Would you want a two door or a four door?"

"Would you see me at 9:00 AM or 10:00 AM?"

It's best to lay it out as if you hardly care.

"Sometime this afternoon or sometime tomorrow, which works best for you?"

THE KEY TO CLOSING

I can go on and on with closing, but a rule of thumb is try to find out the 'key' feature or benefit they are looking for. There may be a 'key objection' they have about your product or service. Once you have this information, the rest of your job is helping them thru the process of justifying the investment. Don't over complicate the selling process. Don't 'Go to combat' on your customer. This is all the leverage you really need. There are so many closing techniques that are downright stupid. For your entertainment, go check them out on You Tube. Look up 'Car closing techniques' or 'Closing techniques'. There are some videos that use hidden cameras. It will make you want to puke.

I have always worried what my customer thinks of my style of selling. I want to be genuine and honest. If you are trying closing techniques, you had better face the fact you can easily loose a great account if they suspect you are manipulating them in any way. You can help them to make a decision, but you better not mislead them. That will be the last time they buy from you. Stick to the principals of integrity and honesty. Help them figure out what they want, and help them get what they expect. Don't leave this earth thinking your job was to manipulate the customer to buy. You will never escape a bad reputation. You are in this for the long haul.

CHAPTER 13

WHY DO YOU KEEP TALKING TO THE WRONG PROSPECTS?

If a prospect says to you "I'll get back to you on that."

What that actually means:

"I'll get back to you in about 5 years on that."

What you think you heard:

"I'll get back to you real soon. I can't wait to use your services. You are the one I've been waiting for"

Your sales manager has told you many times how he 'believes in you' and knows you can 'get the big accounts'. He's so excited about your potential, he can hardly stand it. There's nothing wrong with targeting big accounts, but it can be the biggest waste of your time if you don't know what you are doing. You need to ask yourself, can my company deliver on large accounts? How are they presently doing with their large accounts? Most companies want the large accounts, but *they are way out of their league to serve them* and guess what, the responsibility gets dumped on the salesperson to solve all the problems and take all the hits. Big accounts require large amounts of your time and resources to maintain. Don't let your sales manager tell you otherwise. I have learned the hard way, that my company could not service the biggest accounts the way they expect to be served. Many bosses and managers just don't acknowledge the challenges that come with these accounts. They think they will be able to deal with anything that comes their way. They don't want to hear about the obstacles. *They want results!* And now!

Hey Boss, I Got a Big Account

I had been working on an account for months. I finally broke through and started getting regular orders. After a couple of months I got an order of $131,000. You'd think my boss would have been ecstatic. Wrong. This just put everyone into a tail spin. My company was not used to getting orders of that size. Just to accept the order, it took about two weeks to figure out how we could process it. My company started negotiating terms and lead times without me. It was a huge lesson on going after large orders. Salespeople are so focused on getting the sale, they often forget the customers' ability to pay should be a consideration. Even if they have the ability, they may have a low credit limit and all the applications need to be updated and checked for good standing. This can take additional weeks to complete. The salespersons job has many phases, and there are many hoops to jump through even before an order can be delivered.

I Never Had a Chance

I'm reminded of a large account I worked so hard to impress. I made many visits and I thought I was making progress just by the number of visits I was able to make. The purchasing person was nice and said he would soon send me an RFQ (Request For Quote). I occasionally dropped an email to say 'hello'. To my disappointment, I never received a call.

It's important to 'qualify' our prospects before we sell to them. What does that mean? I'm glad you asked. A purchasing person is not necessarily going to give you any information about your competitor if you don't ask. If you are attempting to sell to a new prospect, you need to find out if there is any potential business to be earned. Just because they let you into their office, does not mean you are making progress. Find out who they are buying from and why. Find out if they actually need what you are offering.

Go forward 2 years... now I am working for the competitor that had the account. I never realized the bond and history that was keeping me from penetrating this account. ***I never had a chance!*** The relationships were over 20 years old. There were deep friendships with several people from both companies. They knew the order desk people, the credit department, and even the delivery drivers. Everyone knew each other. There was a VMI (Vendor Managed Inventory) stocking program implemented. Not in a million years would I have a chance of any portion of their business. (Maybe an emergency situation, but that's it.) It made me realize I did not qualify this account at all. Boy was I barking up the wrong tree! I had no idea I was asking the *wrong* questions all along and the purchasing person was never going to give me an order anyway. My lack of experience was killing me. I needed some re-evaluating. Don't ever think you have enough knowledge that you can relax. Great achievers are addicted to improvement. They are always asking: How can I do better? What am I doing wrong? Who can I talk to about this?

STOP LOSING YOUR GOOD CUSTOMERS

Each year the average business loses approximately 14% of their customers.

https://www.linkedin.com/pulse/each-year-youll-lose-14-your-customers-rotha-chan [Source: BusinessBrief.com] also https://blog.hubspot.com/sales/sales-statistics

I'm certain this number varies greatly on the type of products or services you sell. (I have also seen a similar statistic go from 10% to 17%) Regardless of the fact, this is an important statistic to think about. I have witnessed this at every company I have worked for. There is a 'churn rate' that seems to be unavoidable. Why is that? Some customers only need you for one transaction. Some only need you for a particular project, and then there are some customers that are not happy about something…what is it? According to American Executive Centers website:

Nearly 70 percent of customers leave as a result of their dissatisfaction with the business' attitude.

http://www.americanexecutivecenters.com/why-your-customers-leave/

I have seen this to be true and I know this to be true. Both you and your company have to be very careful how you deal with your customers. The 'churn rate' of your company might be revealing the health of your company. No doubt, there are some customers you should lose.

Maybe it's time to address this subject in a company meeting. Just by changing the *perception* of your company's attitude, could make a huge impact. Efforts to improve customer experience can be discussed. You could look at the specific areas of your company that you think customers are most dissatisfied. Maybe it is a specific person in the company that is causing a lot of the issues. You want to keep the right customers.

As I look back, I can remember that *every* company I have worked at has had a reputation of being *difficult with their customers*. Maybe it's the inherent nature of running a business and keeping it profitable. But to me, it only proves the value of a good sales person goes beyond just writing an order. The sales person must create the perception of a caring company, even when there is no love there. The statistic reveals that some customers are feeling they are not appreciated at all. I know it is always in the interest to keep every customer satisfied; however I also know it is impossible to please everyone.

76% of consumers say they view customer service as the true test of how much a company values them.

– Aspect Consumer Experience Survey   http://www.business2community.com/strategy/6-times-expensive-win-new-customer-retain-existing-one-01483871#sy0hMYJyMDHOmusS.99

It is 6 Times more expensive to win a new customer than to retain an existing one.

http://www.business2community.com/strategy/6-times-expensive-win-new-customer-retain-existing-one-01483871#sy0hMYJyMDHOmusS.99

Is this a good statistic? You bet it is. It takes a lot of time to gain a loyal customer. You may get an order or two from some new accounts, but what you are after is the repeat customer. That is where we find the most profit. Each transaction becomes less labor-intensive to process and you are broadening your opportunities to sell more products or services. Some accounts require a large investment of your time to earn their business. Pick your prospects wisely.

PROSPECTING

How can you find new customers? Many sales people do little or no prospecting at all. Most companies have no idea on how to prospect to get results that work. There were times when I was so busy with leads and new customers popping up everywhere, I had no need to prospect. However, today the competition is as aggressive as they can be and everyone is fighting to maintain their customer base. Remember you are always losing customers, but so is your competition. This is exactly why prospecting should be a *continual daily exercise.* Customers are always looking for ways to survive and sometimes spreading their purchasing to multiple suppliers, is one way to help their cash flow.

I do believe it is the responsibility of your company to do what they can to provide you with qualified leads, but I know some of them believe it is the 'sales persons' responsibility. Many companies refuse to do any advertising because of the costs and they think they have no responsibility in the success of their sales staff. They are only interested in what's in it for them. This is not a win-win philosophy and is a true reflection of the company you work for. This being said, it is why sales people expect to be paid in direct proportion to the amount of service they provide a company. Don't take any guff if your company says you are making too much money.

I think many sales people dread the idea of prospecting because *it is the area you are most likely to get rejected.* Unfortunately, if you refuse to prospect, you will eventually find your income dwindling. As I mentioned earlier, customers are not looking for you. *You have to look for them.* You have to bring them into your company by letting them know you exist and are willing to work hard to earn their business. You have to learn to prospect so you can produce results that pay off. If this is not your style, then maybe you are 'too soft' for outside sales.

Prospecting is searching, exploring and hunting for potential customers. There are a lot of different ways to do it. Sometimes they work great and other times you might have to try something else. Whatever seems to work for you is good, until it's not. Emailing, inbound marketing, networking, trade shows and cold calling are what I use. Referrals are always the best. Remember, you are looking for qualified prospects.

How I Produced the Greatest Results

Let me tell you about a little secret that works very well for me. It is simple and it works. I have used this for many years and this has produced the greatest results of anything I have ever tried.

I use Google Maps. Follow me step by step and watch the results.

- Pull up Google Maps.

- Type in the search box an industry you service. Example: General Contractors
- <u>Now add the zip code or the name of the area you wish to prospect at the end of it</u>. Example: General Contractors 92021 and push search.

BOOM! You will be able to see all the GC's in that area. Just 'zoom in' to the area you want to see. You will also get to click on the red dot and get a lot of information on them. Even get to see their facility. You can quickly identify if it is a residence or a medium sized company. It leads you to their website, etc. These are not dead leads. These are *active* companies that are showing up on the Google search because they are legit. They have websites. They are open for business. They are waiting for you to visit them. You can also move the map around to different areas with your mouse.

Now let's say you specialize in selling to 'Cabinet Manufacturers.' Type in: Cabinet Manufacturers 92701 and push search.

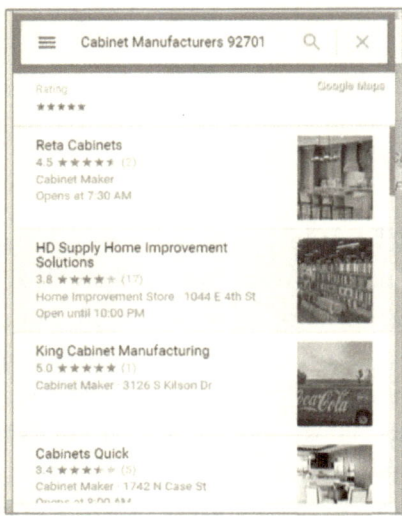

You can see their reviews and learn a lot about them. Read the reviews for names of key individuals to contact. This is a gold-mine of information!

Now let's say you sell to the manufacturing industry. In particular you sell Stainless Steel tubing. You might search this: Stainless Steel Fabricator Los Angeles

Gold-Mine! All the companies you should know about, but don't.

Another trick I learned, changing the wording will often bring up companies that did not show up on the first search.

For Example: Stainless Fabricator Los Angeles, instead of Stainless STEEL Fabricator. So, this tells you, *the more creative you get with your search wording, the better your results will be.* I have been able to find companies that were hidden gems for years! Remember, don't tell anyone about these tricks. It will keep you one step ahead of the competition.

TAKE THE LONG WAY HOME

I want you to know that many times I stumble across a company when I'm just driving around. I would make it a habit to go thru as many business parks as I could on the way home. This was very fruitful. Many companies even have their facility doors open and you can quickly see if they do something you might be interested in. If they looked good, I would pull over and look them up on Google to see their website. If that looked good, I would go to the receptionist desk with nothing more than a business card. Here is how I would approach her. (I already discussed this in the chapter called 'Now, let's make that sales call.')

"Hello, I'm not here to see anyone. (Act as if you are a little bit lost.)

"I would like to know, what is the *proper procedure* to contact the purchasing person?"

Many times she would give me their name and email address right on the spot! This works great.

The more people you can see 'face to face' the better the odds are that you will have major breakthroughs in your selling career. Try this, you will get results that will surprise you.

START-UP COMPANIES

Another thing I discovered is 'start-up' companies are a great place to sell products. This is a fantastic opportunity to get with a new company that is open to ideas. How did I find them? Well I discovered that most large cities have a localized 'Business

Journal' Magazine published in their area. Most of the stories in the Journal are about growing companies. Read it, you will find the new companies before your competition.

E Mail

This is an amazing statistic. It goes to show if your email efforts have ceased to give you good results, you need to look at it again.

> *Email is 40 times more effective at getting new customers than Facebook and Twitter combined.*
> — McKinsey   http://www.mckinsey.com/business-functions/marketing-and-sales

There have been many studies that reveal why some email programs are very successful and others are not. You will benefit greatly just by learning one key thing. The **subject line** is the most important part of the email. That was news to me. Once I realized this, I began to notice the emails that I ignored versus the ones I opened. It was true. If the subject line was lame or typical, I deleted it before opening.

> *35% of email recipients open email based on the subject line and nothing else.*   Source: http://sumo.ly/4Cye

They say the average attention span of an internet user is just 8 seconds. That means you had better study how to get their attention, and track your results. Once you learn this secret you will get results. This should affect all your daily emails too.

Personalization is the secret.

Personalizing communications and content makes the difference. No generic headlines. Using emotion is a good thing to consider. Remember, people buy emotionally and they also react to emails that have an emotional subject. Write with candor. Keep them short. Here are some examples:

Hey Bob, Thought you would be interested in this.

Mary, we made a change at Smith Brothers.

Can you join us for a BBQ lunch?

Marty, I think we can save you a lot of money.

Hey Frank, I came across your website and thought we should talk.

Hi Sandra, We are presently supplying many companies in your industry.

We murder termites and bugs fast.

Learn about your prospect before you send an email. It will help you with your subject line. The best way to approach the subject is to *solve one of their problems.*

Research has revealed that you should not use words like: only, free, report, learn, today, win, get, register, Fw: Re:

Never make a **subject line** sound like a sales pitch or anything resembling selling. The content of the email should be short and specifically designed to educate your prospect. You want them to eventually click to your website to find out more.

Voice Mail

80% of calls go to voicemail, and 90% of first-time voicemails are never returned.

www.ringlead.com/25-sales-outreach-statistics-help-sell-better

I have never liked to leave messages on a voice mail, especially to a prospect I do not know. If you do, keep it short. I have no advice about voice mails as it is not anything I am interested in. I personally *never* respond to a stranger leaving a message on my phone. If you know of any great techniques that actually work, call me and leave me a message.

CHAPTER 14

RELATIONSHIPS TRUMP PRICE, EVERY TIME, EVERY DAY, ALL DAY LONG.

But this trend is beginning to change.

Sandy had been in sales for 2 years and decided to buy her first book on selling. She was so excited to discover her problem. The book told her she needed to learn some techniques to 'close the deal'. She concluded the competition must be better at 'closing' than her. So she set out to get armed with a few psychological 'closing' techniques that would disarm the customer, put them in a spell, and get them to agree to buying, when they least expected it.

Sandy is now very successful at her hostess job in a local country kitchen.

Good relationships trump price Every Time

This has to be the most hated truth there is. Why is that? Because, people buy from people they like and trust. That's when a sales rep reveals great value to his company. Many times the initial visit with a prospect is only about price, but later on, that no longer becomes the deciding factor. I have had the awesome experience of having many of my customers follow me to a new job throughout my sales career. It is the most gratifying feeling and proves my premise...that most times, relationships trump everything.

I have heard many sales professionals say "you have to master the right closing techniques, the right intro, the right presentation, etc." They *rarely* say develop a relationship first. Yes, you want to get your customers to buy, but we are here for the long haul. I say, work on your relationships and you won't have to use all those crazy 'closing techniques'.

Your best chance for long-term growth and success is by developing strong working relationships.

The reason you cannot penetrate most large companies is because of the relationship barrier they have with their existing suppliers.

No closing technique, no sales gimmick, no statistical chart patterns will have any effect. Accept the fact that they have been doing business with other suppliers long before you showed up with your big smile.

I know it doesn't make any sense; after all you may have knowledge that you could save this prospect thousands upon thousands of dollars if they would just give you a chance. Sorry, the *relationship* they have with your competition trumps your logic and they don't care about what you have to offer. To them, at this point, *it's not about the money.* It's about their feelings. They 'feel good' about buying from their current supplier. That's exactly what *you* want... loyalty to *your brand* of selling.

I'm not saying you cannot sell to them. I am saying it's going to be a steep uphill climb.

You might have to convince them over time, it **'is'** about the money. In the meantime, you are not going to get the whole enchilada; you might just have to settle for the rice and beans. Relationships can take a lot of time to develop.

98% of the top sales professionals say 'relationships' are the most important part of generating new business

www.business2community.com/social-selling/4-surprising-social-selling-stats-might-change-sales-strategy

Important note: If a large account 'out of the blue' starts calling you, it could be because one of two reasons:

1. They are having difficulty with their present supplier or

2. They are having major financial problems. Be careful. Figure it out. It may not be because of your magnetic personality.

Breaking the 'Relationship' Lock Hold

As I have mentioned, relationships are 'golden,' but there is a factor that is moving the needle in another direction. This is a game changer.

Many companies have recently changed their style to 'On Demand Purchasing'. They are waiting until the *last minute* to purchase products. This is because of 'cash flow' and the fact that things are changing from 'moment to moment'. Manufacturing is constantly tweaking their products on the spot. Customers know they can get products for their production 'faster than ever before'. This is not a 'new' revelation, but amazing suppliers that are now carrying *deeper inventories than ever* before and a huge selection, have taught them this.

If your company cannot respond fast enough to your customers' needs... ***your 'relationship' is no longer a factor in the ordering process.***

This can be great news when it comes to prospecting accounts that you have never been able to penetrate. It can be bad news to accounts that you think you own. Availability and speed of processing orders are the two game changers that all companies have to address in this new market place. Ignore this at your peril.

THE 'TURN OVER' IN PURCHASING

As it turns out, there is a large 'turn over' in the purchasing world, and in the sales world. You should never give up on an account that you desire to have. You will be constantly adjusting your customer/contact list because of changes in personnel. This has been the case over and over again throughout my career. Many purchasing people get promoted to different positions or they move on to new companies. If your prospect now has a new purchasing person, it's time to show up and begin to earn your living. You will never know of the changes out in 'the field' if you aren't checking in once in a while.

Stay in contact with the good accounts.

This is also true when your competition loses their sales rep. Your prospect will finally be happy to hear what you can do for them. Keep your hand 'on the pulse' of what is happening in your territory at all times. You will discover opportunities at unlikely times. Sometimes orders will be thrown on your lap. Stay visible out there.

WHEN THE ECONOMY STARTS TO HEAT UP AGAIN

The one thing you need to be prepared for is the surge of complaints that come when the price of the products you are offering start to go up. In a slow economy most companies refuse to raise prices for fear of losing any customers. This can only last for so long. After the economic conditions get going in the other direction, a flood of suppliers begin to raise their prices across the board. They might of had to wait years for the right opportunity to get those prices up. Your customers will definitely begin to notice, and you had better be on your game as to how you will answer them. Even the most loyal customers will check your pricing with the competition if the *percentage* of increase is too large.

I recommend you save copies of all the emails that alert you to the price increases you have to pass on to your customers. You need to share these notices with your good customers so they can understand the conditions in the market place. This is when you are most likely to benefit from a close relationship with your customer as they will be more adept to believe and trust you. Be aware that many suppliers are slow to increase their prices because they fear being the first on the block with the higher numbers. Smart suppliers anticipate the increases and carry more inventory of the top selling items so they can be last at raising their prices. You need to be quick to take care of a customer that thinks he is getting gouged. It may be necessary to lower your profit margins with some customers while the transition is taking place. Eventually the price has to go up. Your customer will have to face the increase even if he has switched to the competition.

Price increases are always difficult for sales people. It just isn't pleasant to put yourself into a conversation that might not turn out in your favor. I have lost customers because of the smallest price increase. If you have taken your career seriously and made it to the PRO Level, you will find that many customers will not leave you even though your prices are higher than the competition. Be the best rep in the field and you will have the best chance of weathering the storms that come from time to time in sales.

Chapter 15

STOP SELLING RICE BY THE GRAIN!

I'm certain you know by now, you want to sell your customer as much product as possible. I know of many companies that are processing orders that are actually *costing* them money to process. In other words, they are losing money so as to not upset their customer. *Yikes!*

You should not have to apologize for making a profit!

You are trying to make a living at this aren't you? Maybe your company is a non-profit organization. Quit training your customer that you can process $5 orders even though your company has a $25 minimum. Yes, there are exceptions to every rule, however losing money on an order better have a good explanation as to why you are doing this. If a small customer is upset that you have minimums for him, set him free. Let him fly like a sparrow right to your competition. Look at the biggest competitors in your industry. I'll bet they are enforcing their minimums. Stop selling in small quantities; increase the minimum so that no one can purchase anything from your company for under a certain dollar amount.

Start doing <u>less</u> of what is losing you money and start doing <u>more</u> of what has been making you money.

Don't Just Be an Order Taker

There's a reason one salesman is always #1 and you are never #1.

Don't just be an order taker... be a profit maker. What does that mean? You need to be asking for the extras. Many sales people fail to sell the higher profit add-ons. Customers aren't getting the opportunity to take full advantage of everything your company has to offer.

A customer once placed an order with me for a set of six foot piano hinges. Once he received his order, he called me and said "Why didn't you sell me the screws?" The lesson learned is, you are often doing your customer a disservice by *not* selling him something he may need. I'm not sure why I failed to add that to his order, but it may be perhaps that my company only sold those screws in 'bulk' and I was afraid to sell him more screws than he would ever need. If he is going to need a drill bit to install your product, you had better ask him if he needs to purchase some drill bits.

You need to be asking for the next order, in advance. Why? It keeps the competition out. If your customer has placed his order 'in advance' for next week, or the next job, the competitor cannot get it. How did I learn this technique? My competition taught this to me.

Revealing what 'differentiates' you from the competition, should be your daily routine. Bring your 'A' game every day and let your customers 'experience' *the best rep out there.*

Bring new products to demonstrate and sell. Don't be afraid to promote the higher priced product. Let them know why you believe it is worth the value. Show them the difference and above all, ask them for the order!

Is Your Prospect Experiencing Any Pain?

Find out what your prospect thinks of your competition. Is there something that he would like you to work on, maybe solve a problem? Is he getting the service he expects? The quality he wants? The one thing that motivates a customer is pain. They need quick solutions to their problems. Find out what areas they struggle with. Ask them if they are interested in saving money? Are they interested in better service? Find out what you can do to save them money?

When you leave your prospects office do they say, "Now there's a good sales representative, he is hungry and motivated." Be consistent, stay inspired and never give up. You are *headed for success* and let everyone see it and feel it. Be driven.

Chapter 16

Don't Under Estimate the Potential of Some Customers.

I have been caught off guard many times over the years underestimating the potential of some of my customers. They turned out to be little gold mines in disguise. There are many young companies that suddenly have a burst of growth. Your sales with them exploded and you did nothing to earn it except be there when they needed you. Watch closely the entrepreneurs that are hungry and have plans on getting big. You usually can spot them hiring more people and using more product. It's the young companies that seemed to be the best investment of my time. They are open to advice and they really need your help. These are the customers that you want to develop relationships with when they are small, and they stay loyal as they get big.

Then there are customers that initially don't sound very interesting, but I found out later on, they have a particular niche in their market place and they are trying to stay *under the radar* as long as possible, to keep anyone from infiltrating on their monopoly.

An employee once told me of a customer that came to pick up items at the will-call counter several days in a row. On a hunch, I made a cold-call. It turned out to be one of those gold mines. I love being the only salesperson that knows about a growing account. Stick your nose in the door of some small businesses. Many times they don't even know you're out there.

CHAPTER 17

NEVER 'TRASH TALK' YOUR COMPETITORS.

Even a fish wouldn't get into trouble if it kept its mouth shut.

You may be very tempted to mention something bad about you competition, but **don't ever do it**, even if your customer is instigating the conversation. Every bad word you say about them says something about you. Your credibility goes down with every jab. When you break credibility with a customer, you lose all the business. It can easily backfire. I once knew a person that just couldn't say anything bad about anyone. I noticed it early in the friendship. The reason it came to my attention is he had more friends than anyone I knew. Some of the friends seemed like losers to me. I asked him one day why he hangs out with so and so. He gave me a shocking response. "He needs friends too." I thought I must be talking to some kind of Gandi. I admired his attitude and never forgot it. You have to dig deep inside yourself to get to the point that you only say nice things about people. Try it, it's not so easy. It's no wonder that he had so many friends.

Sales people have to learn to 'tame the tongue'. You cannot afford the luxury of saying everything that comes into your mind. You'll be much better off as a person anyway. Focus on the positive, resist being negative. It's better to be remembered for being a positive, upbeat person than for being a person who said everything that came into his warped mind. It is very difficult to listen to a negative person. You can only take so much of it.

NEVER INTERRUPT A SALES CALL
If you happen to show up at a customer and discover there is another salesperson already there, *never* interrupt their business. Don't even wait for 2 minutes. Make a small wave, apologize, and say I'll catch you at another time. This cannot be emphasized enough. You never want to put your customer in a compromising position. Do not make them accommodate your bad timing. Be respectful, and get out as soon as possible. It would be considered extremely unprofessional to stick around. Sad but true, I have been interrupted by other sales geeks about 30 times in my career. It is shocking to have a sales person attempt to make a sales call when I was standing right there with the customer. What are they thinking? It shows the lack of integrity and experience on their behalf. There was one time when the sales guy actually high-jacked my time and acted as if I was not there at all. I cut in and mentioned I was not finished with my visit. So the guy actually said, "Go ahead and finish, I'll wait here." Good grief, give me a bucket.

CHAPTER 18

Life isn't fair... better get used to it.

Oh boy, here we go. You are going to have to learn to 'suck it up' if you want to do well in life, but especially in the selling profession. Are you with me?

I can't tell you how many times I have had to 'bite my tongue' to keep from telling a good customer what I really think. Customers will let you down. They will use you and abuse you. They will distort the truth. They will let you down. Did I already say that? Well get over it, it happens so often they do it over and over again. They will let you down. Unfortunately it becomes the norm. Get used to it. Your competitors are dealing with the same stuff.

I often get together with manufacturers reps to have lunch. We talk about our customers. We discovered we had many of the same customers, but we sold them different products or services. Low and behold, the stories were exactly the same. Bob was a jerk to everyone... it wasn't just me! Bob thought it was his job to keep sales reps humble and miserable. If you want to do business with Bob the tormentor, you had to put up with all his baggage.

Sales people are always under pressure from their own company. They are never completely satisfied with your performance. They always want more! More sales, more profit, more hours, more leads, more success stories, more customers. They don't want to hear your complaints or about your *needs*. This is normal, really. There is nothing unusual about this. Unfortunately, the excrement always eventually ends up at the sales department... and it seems to stay there! It stinks up the whole place. Your company has to make a profit. It's like a monster that has to be fed. It's always hungry for more. Expenses are always going up. Insurance, workers compensation, rent, labor, phone bills, people want vacations, things going South. A delivery truck just blew up. An employee just quit. A customer is suing over something. Are the employees going to get a Christmas bonus this year? What about profit sharing? We need a new computer system... now.

The only way to feed the monster that wants to be fed is to *keep the pressure on the sales department*. Get used to it. It's part of the job. To put in a word of encouragement at this point is warranted... it's really the only bad part of the job. If you keep your head on straight, you can learn to navigate through these obstacles. Yes, it sucks. Yes, you will feel terrible and you might even think of quitting. Don't. Stay motivated, get inspired, be consistent. You have to have a winner's mentality. There is no easy street. Your company needs you to put up with this psycho stuff because they need you and you need them. It's one of those weird love relationships.

You have to learn to separate yourself from your emotions, and realize your company is not any different from any other successful company. This is a survival technique that you *must master*. Your attitude about all of this can be your biggest obstacle in life. No one is responsible for your success but you. Stop putting the blame on everything you can think of. It may be true that some things are not 'right' at your company for you to be successful. Perhaps the company you are working for is not a good fit, but until things change, you have to 'suck it up'!

There are three types of sales people:

-Those that *MAKE IT HAPPEN*

-Those that *WATCH IT HAPPEN*

-Those that say… *WHAT HAPPENED?*

The fact is, your company also has to overlook a lot of things about their employees. Jeff is always late. Mary calls in sick on Mondays and Fridays. Bob has personal hygiene problems. Armando is always unhappy. Steve is fighting with Frank. Mario, the delivery driver, just got a DUI. Linda the accounting girl, just found out she's pregnant. Kim is going thru menopause. Mike is going thru menopause.

Outside sales is a wonderful job! Everyone should be forced to try it so they can understand what it's really like.

I believe criminals should be given a choice… 1 year in prison or 1 year in outside sales.

CHAPTER 19

START LEARNING ABOUT YOUR COMPETITION

Good grief. You hardly know anything about your competition. The only thing you do know is they are kicking your butt all over the place.

You should be studying your competition more. Do you think a professional boxer would go into a fight without carefully studying his opponents' weaknesses and strengths? There is so much to learn, like why aren't you getting some of the best customers?

The fact is...in most sales opportunities, you are not trying to find NEW customers you are actually trying to switch existing customers from your competition.

A new customer is a 'start-up company' that needs materials to make something. They just opened up for business. They need everything. A new customer is someone that is buying your product or service for the first time.

You, on the other hand, are in the business of *switching customers to your company*, or keeping them from going to your competition. That's why you need knowledge, the more the better. Notice I did not say you need 'ammunition' against your competition. You *never* want to blast your competition with negative talk. That's what unprofessional, inexperienced, sales people do. It took me a long time to learn this lesson. It was a huge mistake I was making for years. There were times when I knew all the trash about the competition and could not resist 'discussing what I knew'. It never generated the positive results I was expecting, and made me feel terrible later on. You always want to respond to negative comments about your competition with a statement like "I'm not sure about that, but I do know we..." Play naive to the negative talk. Brush it off, and turn it into an opportunity to show your integrity.

Always 'pass' on the opportunity to 'trash talk' your competition.

So, what kind of knowledge are you looking for? The kind of knowledge that separates you from your competition. What if you find out they are better than you in every way? Then you need to sell 'yourself,' and you have to become 'the difference'. People buy from people. Your style, your 'brand' has to 'stand out' to peak their interest. You can learn a lot about your own company by studying the competition.

GAINING KNOWLEDGE ABOUT YOUR COMPETITOR

Go to their website and look. "Wow, I never knew they sold those. Look at all that stuff."

Ask one of your customers about them. What are their delivery charges? Do they deliver every day of the week? Do they have minimums for free delivery? What is their return policy? What product lines do they carry? Most importantly, ask your customers or prospects **what they like about them?** Find out about their sales person. Why do they buy from him? How long has he/she been there? How often does he stop by? What days does he stop by? What do they dislike about them? How often do they buy from them? Do they offer same day delivery? Do they have 'loyalty programs' to save money? Are the products they offer equal in quality to yours? Do they advertise? Do they have flyers that promote them? Have you seen their flyers? Are the flyers posted on their website? Do they have a catalog on their website? Do they have promotional lunches? Is the company American owned? Are their products warranted? Have you actually seen the competitors' product with your own eyes? Have you touched it, tasted it, and smelled it? Do they have restocking charges? How deep is their inventory? How big is their selection? Do they have other branches? Are some products being shipped from other branches? Do they change their prices all the time? Do they do 'combo' pricing?

Remember, your competitors are also adjusting to the new trends and *are planning to leave you in the dust.* It may be happening right now, while you are reading this book. You are sitting here asking yourself, *"Why aren't we making headway in my territory?"* They are getting set up to *dominate your market.*

You may find your company is lacking in every aspect. You are more expensive, less flexible, less selection, slower to process orders, high error rates, weak looking website, weak looking logo, grumpy order desk people, tough on the customers, strict on company policies, lousy literature, slow truck deliveries, and a bad reputation. Why are you there? I have found in my career that most companies have 'some' of these traits but rarely 'all' of these traits. There is no perfect company. As in everything in life, you work with what you get. If you keep your head on straight, you can find the positive in your company and begin to build on that. This is the key and the **most important thing to think about:**

> There is a reason your company is in business and you need to discover why people are buying from you... and make that your main focus.

-Why does your company have loyal customers?
-Why do you have any customers at all?
-What is it that your customers like about your company?
-Who do they like to deal with on the phone?
-How often do they buy from you?
-Do they buy everything from you, or only a few things?

The answers to these questions will provide you with a wealth of information that can be the starting point of your approach. You may have never looked at the actual reasons your company is making money. You may be relying too much on your 'typical' selling points. Maybe it's because your company opens earlier and stays open later than your competitor. Perhaps your 'quick follow-up' on quotes is what they like best or the better terms you offer on large purchases. Get this information figured out and use the results in your daily presentations.

Chapter 20

Increase Your Odds of Success 100% by Getting Out of Bed

You can't teach people to be lazy -either they have it, or they don't.
                                                    -Dagwood Bumstead

Is Laziness Your Real Problem?

Maybe your problem is you are just not motivated to sell anymore. Indeed, selling can get to you after a while. You need to think about the consequences of not pushing through your pain. Every sales person has hit a wall or two in their career. You simply have to fight back. If you go too long without hard work, poverty will sneak up on you so fast you could easily be unemployed and in trouble. According to a recent survey:

Nearly 80 percent of Americans are living paycheck to paycheck. - CareerBuilder. http://www.newsmax.com/Newsfront/americans-live-paycheck-to-paycheck/2017/08/24/id/809486/

Chances are you are one of those 80%, right? The good news is you are reading this book, and that means there is great hope. The selling profession will bring you an *'above average'* income if you are with the right company. And it will bring you an income *'way above average'* if you learn to hustle. Every type of job eventually becomes a struggle. No matter what job you do, there will be things about it that you do not like. Even rock stars get tired of touring, smoking pot and writing music. Selling is the one job that can give you bonuses and commissions that boost your income. You can see the results of hard work on your paycheck. Most occupations have absolutely *no way to earn a bonus.* They have to wait a year to get a measly raise. You can give yourself a raise by working harder or smarter. Both methods work.

Everything goes in cycles. The tide comes in and the tide goes out. Summer comes and summer goes away. A flower blooms and then it goes away. Another flower blooms to take its place. These are the things that are part of life. This is also true with your selling cycles. You will have times of great prosperity and there will be seasons of dry activity. *This is the norm.* Every place I have worked at seemed to think 'dry periods in sales meant that there was something wrong, and you should be pushed thru this with stern talking. I am telling you from an experienced veteran of over 30 years in outside sales...**you will have dry seasons just as often as all the other great, successful people do.** If your boss does not recognize that, then I would say he is woefully inexperienced, and his pressure techniques on you are nothing short of abuse! I would say he is creating a 'hostile' environment in which to work and this can make things worse. Dry periods do not necessarily mean something is wrong. You cannot force people to buy. You cannot create an opportunity overnight. Things take time to work themselves out. If he cannot understand this, maybe the place you are working is just not a 'good fit'.

If you think you are going to have an increase after increase, month after month, up and up and up, you need to get counseling. Look at any stock on the New York Stock Exchange. Show me one stock that just goes up without a 'pullback' or correction. There isn't even one! How foolish it is to think you will constantly be increasing sales without a slow period. Yes, you can expect an overall up-trend in your sales over a length of time, but this is dependent on the product line you represent. If you sell swimming pools or solar-power systems your cycles will not be constantly up.

Yes, you will have times of personal struggle. You might be dealing with marriage problems or health problems or financial issues. These things can get in the way of your selling. Your car might need expensive repairs. You might need dental work you can't afford. These are also cycles. Don't lose heart. You will get thru this too. If and when you find yourself in one of these periods, then it's time to read a good book on selling. Don't allow yourself to go into a complete depression. You must chose to fight your way back to a healthy lifestyle.

I can tell you what has carried me thru the difficult times… all the motivational books, CDs and seminars I have invested in.

Everyone needs to be reminded they are not alone. Occasionally we need to be 'lifted up' and encouraged. Sometimes you will find that your own company has let you down tremendously. *They* may have caused a slow period in your territory and you know your boss doesn't want to hear you mention a word about it. You need a trusted advisor and partner who knows your business and understands how to help you achieve your goals. Find your advisor in a good 'selling' or 'motivational' book. Chances are your boss will *not* have the right intuition on what to say to you. He is too focused on himself and his own personal issues. He really can't relate to your problems. *Most bosses have never been in 'outside sales' anyway.* Ask another sales friend to recommend a great book he has read. Get back up and dust yourself off! You have a life to live, begin to embrace it. Here's a good book to read by Larry Winget, called *Grow a Pair: How to Stop Being a Victim and Take Back Your Life, Your Business, and Your Sanity*. Go buy it now.

You can do so much more than you think you can. I guarantee, you have a lot more in the tank. Look at anyone that has ever achieved greatness. They did it by believing in themselves first. Then they got a **coach** to get them to new levels of greatness. Your coach is going to be books, You Tube videos and seminars.

You will never find yourself at the top of Mt. Everest by accident.

Find something to achieve in life, and go for it. You don't have to conquer big things. Try little things first. Get vision. Follow people that have blazed the trail before you. They can show you how to do it with the least amount of problems. You can learn from their experience. It can save you thousands of dollars and years of wasted time. Buy a book today. Get up and *'run'*.

Success is not the result of spontaneous combustion. You must set yourself on fire. -Fred Shero   Legendary NHL hockey coach

Chapter 21

How to Destroy Your Territory in 3 Easy Steps

Your mouth... it's not closing enough.
NEVER trash talk, about another customer. Give your lips a break. Many customers know each other, and you can easily ruin two relationships at once. I have discovered, that a territory may be stretched out by large distances, but there are many accounts that were business partners at one time or another. It is surprising how often I learned that a customer was already familiar with a story I was telling. Use your words with restraint. 'Even a fool is thought wise if he keeps silent.' (Proverbs 17:28)

Don't try to make too much profit.

This sounds like a conflict because I thought it was our goal to try and make as much money as possible?

If your customer, that trusts you, finds out by checking with another competitor that you have seriously taken advantage of him, you are going to have a problem. You have ruined your bond and integrity. It is very likely you will never be able to gain it back. You have now opened the door for the next sales person to come on in. There is nothing wrong in making a profit, after all, that is why you are in business, but don't price something so high that you will regret it if a competitor were to get a chance to quote the same product. Once a customer realizes you are the kind of person that tried to do it once, he will never be able to forget it. He may even look back at all old orders and calculate how much you have taken advantage of him. This can cause severe damage to your reputation out in the field.

Never tell your 'jerk' customer what you really think about him.

You cannot secure an order if you just told your customer he is dead wrong and a jerk. It may be true, but he will not believe you. This is a very bad closing technique. Quickly try using a different technique.

Every territory has its jerk customers. It seems there is a large ratio out there. I have discovered, they are usually the very small customers, with very big needs. They often have healthy egos and dislike sales people. They often delight in sharing their own opinion to the world. Even though you could care less if they never call you again, don't allow your emotions the opportunity to get you. They most likely know someone you know. You don't want to be the topic of conversation. Why ruin your whole day over a knucklehead? Move on.

'He who guards his mouth and his tongue keeps himself from calamity.' (Proverbs 21:23)

It takes a great deal of time to develop a territory that produces good numbers day in and day out. It only takes a 'short time' for things to turn bad with an account. The smallest thing can be blown out of proportion. Some orders go from bad to worse. Every order must be baby-sat. Make certain that if a customer had a bad experience on his last order that the next one goes through without a hitch. Remember you are not here to have a great base of friends; you are here to make money. Don't get upset if your money is coming from jerks. Learn to disconnect your emotions from your tough customers. Stay as focused as possible. You will *always* have tough customers in your selling carrier. The sooner you learn to keep your mouth shut and take their orders, the better off you will be.

Another thing that is out of your control is the economy. I have made it through two recessions. The only way you can protect yourself from struggling, is to have enough customers so the impact is at a bare minimum. That is why I believe a continual effort of prospecting is necessary and the only way to maintain your income. Focus on keeping your top producing customers happy and loyal. Stay on your 'A' game.

Chapter 22

Purchasing People

How you see a purchasing person and how they see you is critical to a successful selling career. It's about *connecting* with the 'mind' of the purchasers thinking. As a salesperson, you need to get in their shoes and understand what they want and how they want it. You have to reason with *their* way of thinking, essentially you are serving them.

Every purchaser has a different 'buying style'. Until you know their style, you have to be protective of the way you are selling to them. Some of these people are aggressive and abusive to their suppliers. You want to know if they are 'cherry pickers' or 'demanding'. You want to know if they are 'honest and trustworthy'. Many 'let you have it' if an order is late. Others are flexible and forgiving.

Purchasing has changed so much in the last few years, because of the internet. Customers have many more options at their disposal. They have become more educated about the products they buy, and are always willing to look elsewhere. They can find alternative places to source things in a heart-beat. Many manufacturers are now selling direct, cutting your company out of the equation.

89 percent of consumers turn to Google, Bing or another search engine to find information on products, services or businesses prior to making purchases

Fleishman-Hillard International Communications
fleishmanhillard.com/2012/01/31/2012-digital-influence-index-shows-internet-as-leading-influence-in-consumer-purchasing-choices/

Many purchasing people have a pushy style. Some have tremendous egos. Learning the style of your customer usually comes fast. Many just want 'the bottom line' and then want to get thru the sale as soon as possible. If you respect *the way they want to 'buy' from you,* and give them their products *how they want it*, you will keep them loyal.

I have discovered that the most difficult purchasing people eventually became some of my most loyal customers. I have learned to deal with them. They know they are difficult, and I like to think they respect a sales person that hangs in there for them. It has given me the privilege of attaining some good accounts that other sales people simply gave up on. Listening is the key here. Even though you know your customer is dead wrong on some things, do not say a word. That is how you 'earn' your orders.

Some accounts simply do not want to see you, or any other salesperson. They want privacy. Hard to believe when you are such a nice person. It may have nothing to do with you. Then again, it may have everything to do with you. Maybe…it's your nose ring.

Some customers want to talk about certain subjects every time you see them, before they will give you the order. Many times you have to hear the same story over and over before they give you the order. This is the game you must learn to play and enjoy if you want to be a PRO. Many customers knew when I came by to see them, I was hoping to get an order and many gave me an order *every time I saw them.*

I had one customer that felt it was always his job to 'chisel me down' as far as I could go. But when I told him "Gee Frank, I can't go any lower, you better purchase that from someone else." That's when he would give me the stinking order.

A Call to a Meeting

I had a large customer send me an email that stated they wanted to have a meeting with me. It had a scheduled date with no options. The email did not give any information as to what the meeting was about.

If your customer initiates a meeting like this, it is usually going to be about pricing. I have learned to never negotiate any pricing or promise anything on a meeting like this. Your objective is to *hear out* what your customer wants, and make them be specific, and then kindly say "I'll look into it and get back to you." *Do not say* "Let me think about it." This is because they might ask, "What do you need to think about?"

When I arrived, they escorted me into a meeting room that was upscale with very nice wood paneling, high ceiling, recessed lighting, with a large flat screen monitor on the wall. The name of my company was already on the monitor. Three people entered the room. One of which was the purchasing person I was familiar with. I knew this was serious business. They introduced themselves and drew my attention to the monitor. They discussed some nice things about my company. As the Power Point presentation continued, they demonstrated their growth with us over the last 4 years. The charts had nice growth pointing up. They discussed the future of their company and what they expected to achieve in the coming year. Then they revealed a graph that demonstrated the commodities market trends. Since they purchased a lot of stainless from us, they said that stainless as a commodity has decreased over 20% in the last 2 years but their pricing has remained the same. They also had a percentage number that they *expected us* to reduce our pricing to. This is not an unusual tactic. It was actually very well done, and would be considered in our profession a *sound and brilliant closing technique.*

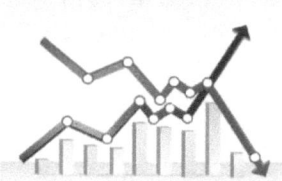

As I mentioned, your objective should only be to *gather information*. I know they expected me to say we would do something to 'fix' this, but I've seen these types of strategies over the years. I think this would have scared a younger company to quickly react and promise 'something would be done immediately.'

Purchasing people from larger companies are being trained how to leverage better pricing from vendors. If you are going to deal with the 'big boys', expect to see this type of tactic. They are spending a lot of money, going to seminars learning how to negotiate better pricing from their suppliers. Why not? Salespeople have had the upper hand for decades.

By giving yourself *time to look into the matter*, you can make better informed decisions. Never rush into an answer until you gather good information. What we discovered was, while the stainless commodity did reduce slightly over the years, *the costs of manufacturing and shipping had actually increased proportionally.*

Lesson Learned:

In business you have to make a profit. If you are not in business to make a profit, then get out! You are ruining it for those that are trying to make a living at it. It is also giving customers *the wrong impression as to the actual costs of supplying that product.* Do your research. Don't make emotional decisions that will come back to bite you later.

CHERRY PICKERS

Every salesperson has to deal with the dreaded 'cherry picker'. This is a purchaser that picks thru your quote and only gives you a small portion of the order. They never let you know in advance they are going to 'nickel and dime' you. You will have to protect your company from these customers. You will always have a hard time making any money from them. I suggest you protect your quotes by putting this on the header:

This quote is contingent on the complete order. All prices are subject to change if any portion of the quote is altered in any way. This quote is good for 30 days.

If a customer has you quote often, and you are not getting the orders, it's time to send them a 'No Quote' on their next RFQ (Request For Quote) You are burning up company resources and they are only using you to keep someone else honest.

A Cheap Date

The customer that shows no loyalty is more trouble than they are worth. This is the type of customer that will come to you weeks after the initial sale and say they found it cheaper somewhere else. Then they will have the nerve to say they want you to credit and rebill them at a lower price or they will take their business elsewhere. Show them the door. A customer that is always trying to negotiate their orders is better off dealing with your competitor. There is nothing wrong with making a profit. These customers are always jumping around from one supplier to another and are very high maintenance. Don't expect to convert them into decent loyal believers of your 'brand'. They are not interested in a long-term relationship; they only want a cheap date.

Am I #1?

Customers have asked me on several occasions, *"How do we rank in your territory?"* What they are saying is, are we on your top 10 list? Why do you think they want to know this? Occasionally a large customer will ask for a favor and say *"Are we too small of an account for you?"*

They want to know where they rank, to use that knowledge as *leverage*. It is an intimidation tactic. I have had some customers ask me over and over to try and get an answer. *"Are we in your top 10, how about your top 5?"* **Never** give this information to your customer. **Never** give out any information that your customer can use against you. **Never** discuss *their* ranking or any other customer ranking. There is no good reason you need to give out that information.

Often times a customer will ask for a list of all their prices. This should raise a red-flag. They can find their prices by going thru their invoices, but they want *you* to create some kind of list for them. I recommend *you never give this information.* It usually leads to bad news. They don't want to do the research themselves, but they need the list to give to competitors. Oh, they will come up with all kinds of good reasons they need the list, and it will never include *"We are shopping for better prices, or we are about to drop you as a vendor."* Do not give out any lists with prices! Stall. Tell them you will look into it. Tell them it's a lot of trouble to the accounting department. If they insist, wait for several weeks, and then come up with a list that has no prices. Do not provide them this information. If you do end up giving them a list, be prepared to hear this, *"I did not know we were paying this much for _____.*

You can always tell them "We never give out lists like that."

NEVER REVEAL YOUR SOURCES

The value of your company is in large part, based on the knowledge it has on sourcing products. Those sources can be called vendors, manufacturers, suppliers and distributors. They should always be kept secret. *Never reveal your sources!* Even with the internet, the source of a particular product may not be found. Protect this information as if it was a crime to reveal it. Most large companies make their employees sign a disclosure agreement to keep their sources confidential. Why is this important? Because it gives you a competitive edge and *you don't want your customer going direct to your source.*

Over the years I have had many examples where I lost a customer because they ended up going direct. At one time I had a great account buying a lot of brass parts. We had a secret source...I thought. What I didn't realize until it was too late, was the part number we assigned to the product included the *vendor part number* in the description. It was obvious it was a unique number. An intelligent purchasing person could easily figure it out. And he did. Good-bye big account.

Another example was a vendor that had their name all over their boxes. We had to receive the product and re-package it to keep the source a secret. For over a year everything went well. Then one day, someone failed to re-package the product and the vendor was revealed. A short time later, my customer informed me he would no longer be buying that product from me as he was buying direct.

Many vendors *promise* they will never go direct to your accounts, but time and time again I have been burned. Don't ever believe they will *never* buy direct, there is always an exception to the rule, and they find great reasons to justify stealing your account. I can think of an account that I had that was doing about $70,000 per month in one product. We had no problem supplying the customer. The manufacturer of the product was interested in the account and asked if they could send out a rep to help me gain more business. I checked with our purchasing department to see if it was a good idea. She said *"Don't worry they would never go direct, we are their biggest customer."* After about four months, I saw an invoice on the desk of my customer. It was from our manufacturer! I acted as if I didn't see it. I immediately called our purchasing department and told them about it. She said *"There is NO WAY on God's green earth that they were dealing direct!"* Well she was wrong. Once it was revealed that it was true, my company immediately dropped the whole line (Worth millions of dollars.) and we switched to a new manufacturer and kicked butt on that greedy dirty manufacturer. It almost put them out of business.

I have many more examples I could share but just let me say this, vendors will tell you they are *loyal*, but I have found *many are not*. You can't blame the purchasing person for trying to find your sources. They want to be a hero at their company and I have found they are often-times sneaking behind your back. Vendors have told me that a customer has *attempted to go direct*.

The trend is *more and more direct business*. It's just part of the free-market in America. Big companies must grow to survive and they must often-times 'cut out the middle man' to stay in the game. It's painful for someone that has invested so much time and money to promote a product, only to have it pulled out from beneath them from a big manufacturer. To make matters worse, these manufacturers never go to the sales person that developed the account and say 'thanks'.

Chapter 23

Eating Crow

If you are hungry for success, you will have to develop a taste for eating 'crow'.

You will need to eat crow when your company serves up a disaster of an order, to a customer you want to keep. There is no way to prepare 'crow' so it will taste good. It is always a humbling experience.

Eating 'crow' is necessary when you realize that you actually said or did something, that your customer has discovered, is not in their best interest. Here are some examples:

-Dropping the ball! You said you would do something and you failed to do it.

-Lying about the approximate price.

Lying about the product quality.

-Over-charging on a product.

-Failing to deliver when promised. Actual lead-time was much longer than originally stated.

Now you have to suck it up and tell it like it is.

> *It is the sales persons' job to "try to save the account".*

How to Apologize

Here are some tips I learned on how to apologize:

1. *Express genuine remorse.* "I'm sorry," or "I apologize for..."
2. *Admit* you or your company made a mistake. Take responsibility for your actions or behavior, and acknowledge what you did. Ouch! You might even say something like "If I had a chance to do it over again, I wish I would have ..." or "I wish I would have done..." Maybe something like, "I know this might have caused you a lot of headaches."
3. *Tell them what you are going to do about it,* or what you already did to fix it.
4. *Promise that as much as it is in your power, this will never happen again.*

It is Very Easy to Lose a Good Customer

It's hard to get them, and so easy to lose them.

Selling is a minefield for *what you say!* It is the single biggest challenge you will discover about yourself. You want to say *what your customer wants to hear.* Even when you know it might be difficult to deliver on your promise. It is better to turn down an order, than to promise something you know could lead into a fiasco down the line. Avoid the land mines. Tell your customer that you would love to have the order, but you know the potential for things to go *'South'* is just too high. Let your customer know, *you would not want to risk the relationship over one order.* This is the behavior of a PRO Sales person. You will not go wrong with the truth.

WHEN YOUR COMPANY MAKES A HORRIBLE DECISION

I was minding my own business. I was a seasoned salesman. I was making the most money I had ever made. The economy was strong. The sun was out. The birds were chirping.

Out of the blue, my company decided it would be a great time to raise the minimum order amount for truck deliveries, from $50 to $100. Now, that is not an unreasonable decision. The amount of business we were doing could easily justify it. What happened next is where everything went wrong.

My customer was easily in the top 3 of the largest accounts in that branch. They purchased products just about every day. The new minimum normally would never affect them. However there was one day my company called me to ask what I wanted to do with an order that had only reached $95. I said "deliver it". The warehouse manager said he can't because "it does not meet the new minimum". I reminded him that the customer had just placed an order for $250 the day before. He said "That was yesterday, today is a different day." Now, as a typical commission salesman, I was not in any mood to deal with this little *"Not going do it"* person. This just didn't make any sense to me. So, I talked to his boss, the branch manager. He was in support of the decision to *'HOLD'* the order until they added another $5 to the order. I asked him "You are not going to ask me to call the customer are you?" He said, *"Yes, it was the principal of the thing. Yes, call the customer."* As I write this, I can hardly believe this actually happened, but it did.

"It's the Principal of the Thing"

So I called the customer, and it just happened that the owner answered the call. He said "Larry, what can I do for you?" I said, "Hi Tom, I just talked to my office and they had mentioned that they were going to make a delivery to your company tomorrow morning, and I was wondering if you needed anything else added to the order." He said "No, we're fine." Then I said, "Well, we have this *new minimum* program for truck deliveries that we are trying to meet and I want to see if I could help them out. Could you just add *anything* to the order, we could easily take care of it." He asked "How far are we from the minimum?" *(Yikes!)* I told him $5. He said, "Cancel the order and come in to see me tomorrow." I knew this wasn't going to go very well.

The next day I strolled up and said "Good Morning Tom." He walked up to me and said, "Larry, don't take this personally, but we are going to take our business elsewhere." He was firm and to the point. "I already placed my $95 order with the competition. They said they would be happy to deliver it." I tried my best to remedy the situation by eating 'crow' but he said these words that I'll never forget... **"Larry, it was the principal of the thing."** Those were the exact words my company said to me, about him. Bye, Bye Large account.

Lesson Learned

I believe the lesson learned here is, that company policies should be considered 'guidelines' not 'the law'. Flexibility should be at the discretion of the sales person, as they are the ones that take the hit, and often times have *no other option* but to be caught in the middle of a company policy and an overzealous manager. It should be acknowledged that the sales person can see the situation from a clearer perspective. They are looking at the financial loss in the 'long term', while the manager is looking at the financial loss in 'the short term'. It is impossible to stumble upon a large account like that, and expect to get their business. To simply 'give it to the competitor' is downright shameful. The customer refused to have any communication with the manager. He told me, anyone that would enforce the $5 issue was not the type of person he would ever want to do business with anyway.

STANDING BEHIND YOUR COMPANY

There will be many times you will have to live with the decisions and company policies that don't make sense to you. We all have to be *loyal* to the company that provides for us. We are there to serve them with the best we have to offer. Stand up for what is right and never compromise on ethical business practices. Stand behind, and represent your employer as if it were your own company. Be the best employee you can be. Sometimes it is necessary to challenge policies that seem to be harming business.

Sorry to say, I have lost many customers to things that were *out of my control to fix*. I once had a very large custom order that had to be delivered no later than a certain date. There was plenty of time to make it happen. I did everything I could to make certain nothing could go wrong. Double-check, triple-check, follow-up call. Well, things went *'South'*, and the product did not ship on time from the vendor. Not only did we lose the customer, but my company had to eat the unwanted late product. It amounted to a huge loss and a horrible experience.

There will be times when your company will ask you to sell a product or service that you do not believe in. Something about it does not sit well with you. The first thing I would do is *challenge the manager to do a ride-along with you.* Say "I want you to show me how it's done". Tell him to demonstrate how a sale of this product should go *in front of a customer.* Demand it. If he refuses… don't sell the product. Never represent an inferior product or service as something other than it is. Your integrity is on the line. Your manager already proved he has no integrity.

Restocking Fees

It is never easy to discuss with your customer that there is going to be a restocking fee on a return. Sometimes you simply cannot get around it. It is important that you stand behind your company on these fees. Why? Because they are necessary to help off-set the expense of all the labor involved in taking a product back. The best way to avoid the pain of charging restocking fees, is to *let your customers know* that all returns (beyond 30 days or?) are subject to restocking fees with no exception. This can be on the invoice or on the quotes etc. They need to understand your company enforces restocking fees.

Going South

Another thing I've seen over and over throughout my career,

Things can go 'South' pretty fast with an account that you think you own.

One day you are the best rep that ever lived, and the next day you are the looser of the century. Things can fall apart that are out of your control. You may find that an emergency shipment never shipped. Maybe your purchasing department got it wrong, or the order was on hold because they were behind in payables. Maybe your competition finally was able to penetrate this account and they are low-balling everything they can quote.

Be ready for trouble at any moment. I guarantee you are going to have unexpected challenges in your best accounts. You've got to be on their mind when they find themselves in trouble. You have to solve their problems as quickly and seamlessly as possible. Keep up with how things are going on a daily basis. Process credits quickly. Return your calls with expediency.

BAD DAYS

There is going to come a time when it seems the whole territory is turning to one big pile of excrement. You've had enough for one day and its only 8 o'clock! What I've learned is salespeople are actually running their own business. They just happen to be doing it under someone else's roof. Yes it's true, you are not taking the same risks or paying the overhead etc., etc., etc., but you are dealing with many of the same 'day to day' problems and having to solve them. The hard part for the salesperson is they have to deal *directly* with the difficult customer *face-to-face*. They are taking the bullets head on. They have to look in the eyes of the customer. They have to 'suck it up' and 'explain' and 'apologize' and 'solve the problem' and then they have to eventually 'go back' to the difficult, disgruntled customer and try to get more business. Good grief, it's no wonder salespeople have all those black and blue marks on their faces.

Some days you have to call a colleague friend and say "Can you meet me for a cup of java. I'm having and excrement day?" and "Can you buy?"

Don't allow yourself to dwell on the negative any longer than is necessary. You cannot go back in time. You can only look forward to the future. Dust yourself off and renew your mind. Force yourself to move beyond the 'nightmare day' and breathe in new hope. You are not alone. Every salesperson has this same experience at one time or another, no matter how hard you try to keep things from falling apart, they fall apart anyway. Keep your brain free of negative stimulus. You can't afford the luxury of dwelling on, and swimming in your sad feelings. No one is attracted to that. It's ugly and only makes it last longer than it needs to. Snap out of it as soon as possible.

The only thing you can really control is how you react to things out of your control.

-Anonymous

CHAPTER 24

GET ORGANIZED.
GOOD GRIEF, WHERE'S YOUR CUSTOMER LIST?

If you want to be average, just keep doing what you've been doing and eventually you will become the best *average salesperson* you can be. If you want to 'run with nothing holding you back', then you need to get organized. Would you go to a dentist that had all his drilling tools lying around everywhere? How about an accountant that had piles and piles of stacked papers laying everywhere? Part of selling your 'value' as a salesperson, is found in looking as professional as possible. The perception of an organized sales rep is one of trust and quality. Don't go into an account with a messy notebook or brief case. Look polished and ready to work. I used to keep all my brochures 'very organized' in the trunk of my car. Many customers asked if they could browse through them to see what else they could get from me. This was a reflection of my professional work ethic. I was happy to let them dig through my trunk. Some wanted to see it on a regular basis. I made certain there were always samples and updated literature to see.

As I mentioned earlier, my customer list was always at an arms distance in my car. I was always using it for information. I even added customer account numbers to the list to help speed up the process when I called in my orders. It became a living breathing document. If I found a prospect while driving around, I would *add it to the list* so I didn't miss them the next time I was in the area. How easy is that? Create systems that work for your leads.

REVIEWING THE BASICS

The greatest achiever in any profession or sport is never done learning. The principals and questions in this book are just as valuable to the veteran as to a beginner. Large companies and great sports teams are often heard saying 'We are going back to the basics that made us great.' That doesn't mean they failed somewhere. It means that 'success' is a refining process that is never completely done. If you think for a second you are too good to review the basics of your profession, you most likely are not one of the top performers at your company.

CHAPTER 25

10 HABITS TO STOP DOING NOW

When you're good at making excuses, it's hard to excel at anything else.   -John L. Mason

If you want to get your *breakthrough*, you have to begin to change your bad habits. These 10 things will help produce higher profits.

1. STOP WASTING TIME WITH LOW-DOLLAR ACCOUNTS

You know these accounts well. They are actually your friends. They don't buy enough to justify all the time you spend with them, but you like them. Time lost is never to be found again. Just by maximizing your time you can increase your income significantly. It doesn't take a big account to double your income. It might just mean adding a few more small accounts. This is something you can do in a relatively short period of time.

Not only are you visiting them too much, you are giving them better pricing than they deserve. You have to decide if you truly want to make money or do you want to have lots of friends. Don't take this hard, but it's the truth. Try to seriously limit your time by starting your visits with, "I've got to keep it short today." Don't be surprised if they say "good". Most likely, they will not mind a bit that you are going to see them less frequently. Be busy with more *new* accounts and less busy with the old low-dollar accounts.

2. STOP GOING INTO ACCOUNTS WITH NO PLAN

If you are just going to stop and visit, that means you have no intention of doing any order writing. What are you, some kind of social consultant? I thought you wanted to increase your income. If you are visiting accounts with no plan or intention, this is a guaranteed way to go no-where... fast. How is it working for you? I do know, if you have *no goals,* you have *no chance* of getting out of your present situation.

Start by thinking what you want to talk about or promote this week. Is it a product or a service you offer? Find out if they are buying items from the competition that they could be buying from you. You need to consider the fact that maybe your technique is slowing you down.

3. STOP DISCOUNTING EVERYTHING

I know you have a hard time selling anything at the suggested price. In fact, you haven't sold anything all year at the *normal price*. You think the customer expects you to *discount everything*. Guess what? You taught them that. Now you're stuck. You know if they find out you are raising your prices they might ask you about it, and golly-gee you simply cannot take the humiliation of telling them the price recently went up. So instead, you continue the bad habit. The best thing you can do at this stage in the game, is to stop seeing that customer and let them call their orders in to the order desk since you are too unprepared to defend your prices. The days you call in sick, are *your* best 'profit' days. The problem lies not with the price, but it is the way you are presenting your *value* to the customer. You are the best thing that ever happened to them.

4. STOP SEEING HIGH-MAINTENANCE LOW-PROFIT ACCOUNTS

There are some accounts you have to "Fire". You have a lot of them. They keep you busy, busy, busy. In fact you don't have much time to follow up on the new leads. (Maybe you should give those new leads to the #1 salesperson because he will find the time to see them.) High-maintenance Low-Profit accounts can take up 80% of your selling time. Every territory has lots of them. This is a test of your intellect and experience, to learn how to gracefully handle these accounts. The difference between you and the #1 salesperson is you have not learned how to *limit your engagement* of these accounts. They have continual problems and needs. Perhaps the reason you have these accounts is because your competitor has determined *they are not worth the time* and gave them over to you. Now you are so busy you don't have time to pursue the good accounts out there. *Seriously limit your engagement* with these time-wasters. Don't offer solutions to *every* problem they have. A lot of the things they want you to do have no ROI, (return on investment). They are used to asking you to do the work for them that takes up *their* time. You do it because somehow you believe that maybe this will turn into something big. I'm not saying don't look for opportunities to turn this *'dog of an account'* into a great account. I am saying... *limit your invitation to do practically anything*. Don't offer to check into things that you already know is not going to be a 'good fit' for your company.

5. STOP TAKING SMALL ORDERS

Oh good grief, you are still taking orders for $20. And delivering them! Maybe you should deliver mail too. Don't be afraid to ask *"Is there anything else we can add to this order, it's not quite close enough to our $100 minimum to process?"* or *"C'mon Bob, don't make me have to explain to the boss why we are taking $20 orders."* Your customer has to be aware of the policy you have toward $20 orders.

Tell them *"I wish I could do it, but it's not my decision. They tell me, we lose money processing $20 orders."*

6. STOP HANGING AROUND WITH NON-PRODUCERS

Don't spend so much time with the slackers of the company. You are starting to sound like them. Act like a top producer. Be the one that appears to be 'headed for success.'

7. STOP STARTING YOUR DAY WITHOUT A GOALS LIST

Are you 'winging' it? Your 'To Do' list only has two things on it! You are seeing the same 20 accounts every week. Get focused and get busy. You have to have a plan to achieve multiple things every day. Each day of activities moves the ball forward. You will accomplish a lot more in one year if you commit to making goals.

8. STOP TALKING ABOUT THE COMPETITION

Don't discuss your competition with your customers if you can avoid it. Sell your own company. You have a lot of good things to say if you do what I discussed in the 'branding' section. Avoid anything that would give your customer a reason to believe you were not a 'top notch' sales person. Sales Pros resist the temptation to get negative.

9. STOP BLAMING OTHERS FOR YOUR PROBLEMS

First you said you were doing so badly because of the recession. OK, I get it. When things were *booming*, you said it was 'the competition'. Now you are blaming your *own* company. When are you going to get around to blaming *yourself?*

Get help by learning what you are doing wrong or not doing. Remember, what you are *not willing to do* is most likely your biggest problem.

10. STOP TALKING SO MUCH

The #1 thing purchasing people complain about is that the sales people *talk too much*. Don't waste their time. Do more listening.

Resist commenting on 'everything'. They really don't want to hear your opinion. By the way, did they ask *"What is your opinion on this?"* I didn't think so.

Ask more questions, give less commentary. I know it is natural for all sales people to be good talkers. It is your gift, but please learn this lesson, you can destroy your career with your tongue. The absolute best sales people do a lot of listening and they do everything they can do to 'guard their tongue'. One bad comment or misrepresentation can change the way you are perceived.

Chapter 26

10 Habits to Start Doing Now

FORMULA FOR SUCCESS

1. Start Your Day With A List Of Customers To Contact

Plan your day. See as many accounts as you can face-to-face. This is your best chance to find opportunities. 'Just-showing-up' increases your odds of making a sale. If you don't have any appointments already set, start your day with the accounts that are 'furthest away'. Statistics show that sales people rarely see the accounts that are distant. See those *first,* and gradually work your way home. By the time you hit your last account, you are almost home.

Commit to being on-time for all your appointments. It is shameful to be a late person. Some people are always late. This shows disrespect to the person you are going to see. If I have a choice, I will discontinue a friendship with a person that is late for everything.

Better three hours too soon, than one minute too late.

-William Shakespeare

2. GET ORGANIZED

I know this sounds so lame and simple but it can be a big boost to be organized. It is very easy to have all your work spread out in your car after all it is your office on wheels. It is a great feeling to have things organized. I don't think you can be nearly as effective when you see the pile of paperwork at your side. Put your 'goals list' on top. Focus on *one thing* each day, and that is seeing all those goals on your list accomplished.

3. START PROSPECTING ON GOOGLE

This is a gold-mine of information. Study the section on prospecting. Often I will look for new customers based on an intuition. Something made me think about an industry I have not explored and I will start to search different phrases with zip codes. This usually pays off with a lead or two to contact. You have to keep the potential prospects coming. It is part of your formula for success. The bigger your 'active' customer base, the better your income. Look for leads in a local business journal magazine or newspaper. There are stories on businesses that are new or have developed new products. If you are selling pool cleaning services, go to google maps type in swimming pools with the zip code you want to prospect. Click on 'satellite' and you can zoom in to see which houses have swimming pools. There are so many ways to get Google maps to help you. Try different things using the zip code you want to prospect in. Look for opportunities everywhere. Google maps can help you no matter what you are selling.

4. Focus on what matters

You've heard of the 80/20 rule. 80% of your business is done by 20% of your customers. This has been studied at for years and has proven to be a very accurate statistic. Take good care of your top 20%. Limit your time with the bottom 80%. *Focus on the customers that can be elevated into your top 20%.* Selling is getting smart about *who* you are going to spend your valuable, limited time on. Manage your time to focus on the most productive thing to be doing at all times. Pro sales people are not spending their time on the small things that produce nothing of value in return.

5. Prepare to raise some prices

C'mon, some of your accounts are getting better prices than they deserve. I know you want to treat them special but as a 'business decision', it is not a good idea. Look for areas where you can increase the 'bottom line'. Most customers know they are paying lower than the market should bear and would not complain if your price went up slightly. You don't have to discount *everything* they buy from you, nor should they expect you to.

6. Go see some accounts you have neglected

If you've been in the field for a year or more, it's time to go see some of those neglected accounts. Often times, things have changed. Maybe the purchasing person has moved on. Maybe they expanded their business and are now growing rapidly. Don't underestimate the potential of some accounts. I have been caught off-guard many times. It is a great idea to keep old leads in a file somewhere. This is a good place to review when your prospecting efforts are not paying off. Timing plays a role in sales. I have had the opportunity to win a customer simply because I happened to show up when they were having difficulty with the competition. Repetition is the answer to prospecting. You will get results if you try. Your odds go way down if you never try.

7. Commit to ask for the order

I know asking for the order can be uncomfortable. It may be the reason you are not #1. Statistics show that it pays to ask for the order. It also shows to your customer that you are there to do business. There is nothing wrong with that. You can tell your customer, "I don't want to be pushy, but I just want to ask, can I count on you for the order?"

8. Review your monthly sales reports

This has to be on your 'to do' list every month. These reports are like looking into an x-ray of your territory. You are looking for accounts that are dying and accounts that are growing. You may also find new accounts that you forgot about. Sales people have to treat their job as if they are in business for themselves. Take responsibility for doing the maintenance on the customer list. These lists are the *best* tool to expose if there is 'trouble ahead'. Your customer may not tell you he has been using your competitor. His sales have been dropping in the last two months, and you never noticed it. It also may reveal that your customer is not paying his bills and has to go elsewhere. Your company has him on a 'credit hold' of some type, and you did not know. If you find a customer placed a very large order for the month, go see him. You might find there is more opportunity ahead.

9. Purchase another motivational book

Don't wait another year before you decide it's time to get motivated again. One good book can change your whole perspective. Keep feeding your brain with good instruction. Don't wait until you are in deep trouble before you seek more wisdom. Dedicate yourself to constant education. Have a book ready to read at your desk.

10. Brand yourself now

Your best chance at creating your own success is a *good reputation*. How you are perceived, is the single most important thing a sales person needs to be concerned about. You need to 'sell yourself' first. Nothing can be more damaging to your career than a bad reputation. Branding yourself is the way. You don't need to tell your customers you are now going to become *'the new you'*. Let them see it and feel it. If they notice it and say something, you have just begun to take your territory to the 'next level'. Creating a professional image will set you apart from the others. *Make certain your Facebook page does not reveal you are someone else.* This can be a deal breaker.

Become the best sales rep in your field. Don't be late for appointments. Begin to follow-up and return your sales calls faster than ever. Pick up your phone and get ready to be of service. Don't let every call go into voicemail. Most people will not leave a message.

Be excited to hear from your customers. Give them the 'little extra' service. Respond to their requests as if you care. Learn their names and help them be successful. All these things justify the higher price for your product or services. Customers will gladly pay for 'solutions' to their problems.

CHAPTER 27

A SLOWING ECONOMY

"We are not going to participate in this recession."

When the economy is booming, everything is upbeat. When things get slow your boss will try to ignore the economic numbers and say things like, *"We are not going to participate in the recession."* This is similar to saying "We are not going to acknowledge the fast approaching hurricane."

This management strategy is very naive. They will often use the 'Get Angry and Turn-Up-The-Pressure' technique. They think, somehow by adding more pressure, the salesperson will eventually submit and admit he was responsible for the economic slow-down. I have seen this type of technique tried many times. All this does, is it breaks the 'spirit' of a man or woman.

THE SMART SALES MANAGER

I think the first thing a smart sales manager should do to solve his dilemma, is to look at the economic numbers at a sales meeting *with all the sales staff present.* Bring it out in the open. Don't act like you haven't noticed the economy is turning down. Don't be a coward. How do you ever expect to gain the trust of your salespeople if you deny the reality of the situation? They know exactly what's going on.

Now you need to *'Admit'* to your people, things are trending lower. Get the S&P 500 projected on the screen and look at how the top 500 companies are trending for the year. If you don't know how to do that, ask one of your salespeople, they can help you. Next, look specifically at other public companies in your industry. How are they trending? Before the sales meeting, ask your top suppliers how all the competition is doing. Let's say that you discover it *is* getting slower. Bring out all the sales numbers on your own company. Are you trending similar to the rest?

Next, *'Encourage'* your team. Let them know they are top notch in the industry. Acknowledge the accomplishments they have achieved in the past. Build them up, even if it hurts.

Now, **"Ask"** them for help. Make it a brainstorming session to see what is possible for them to help offset the trend. Don't beat them up! *Let them be part of the solution.* Work as a team. Get them motivated to solve the problem. Everyone needs to **row** the outrigger together, going in the same direction. A sales manager should be top notch and ***intelligent.*** Not just someone that thinks he is something special and actually thinks that 'beating the sales team into submission' is the winning solution. *Be a leader not a beater.*

-Admit

-Encourage

-Ask

-Row

By the way, I *insist* that the sales manager get *himself* into the boat and ***row*** with the rest of the sales staff. This is everyone's problem. No pencil pushers here. Get out from behind your desk and work for a change, you slacker manager! ***"Row"***

There, I said it.

SELLING AT THE PRO LEVEL

Chapter 28

Are you working for the right company? Is your company dying a slow death?

Fred has been in outside sales for 5 years. He has not been able to increase his sales for the last 2 years. He has ignored the most important rule for a sales person. Get out...if your company does not want to grow any bigger than it is.

If you are in sales, you want to be with a company that is 'on the move'. A company that is striving for innovation, and is willing to try new approaches to marketing and committed to the best website they can afford.

Here are some questions you might ask yourself:

-Are they going to be morphing into a greater company in the next 5 years?

-What are their future plans?

-Will they listen and implement suggestions from their sales staff?

-Is their business approach outdated?

-Is the company making money?

-Is the company loosing lots of money?

-How do they treat their employees?

-Is there a lot of turnover in employees?

-How do they treat their sales staff?

It is important for a company to support their outside sales force with the following:

-Encouragement

-Leads

-Professional looking literature

-New products

-Professional looking business cards

You cannot turn a dead company into a thriving company, without the basics. A simple professional website is absolutely necessary. If they do not have any website, run for the door, I mean it. If this company believes 'marketing and tech trends' don't apply to them...this is sign of a dying company.

Ecommerce is growing 23% year-over-year, yet 46% of American small businesses do not have a website.
https://www.bigcommerce.com/blog/ecommerce-trends/

Selling is a very difficult profession and if you aren't supplied with the basics, it becomes impossible to get ahead. Is your competition cleaning your clock?

-They have it all.

You have nothing.

-Their literature puts your company to shame.

You haven't had a new flyer in over a year.

-They have a nice logo.

You have an old logo. Your business cards haven't been updated in 15 years.

-They have new products.

You have nothing new.

If this is reflective of your company, do something about changing those conditions or get out.

You know you are no longer #1, when you begin to smell like #2.

Chapter 29

An Exceptional Opportunity

A cabinet maker had just received the saw blades he had professionally sharpened. He was excited to replace the dull one he had been using, and start using the newly sharpened blade on his new project. After adjusting the height, he turned on the saw and began to push a piece of ¾" melamine through the blade. He noticed the cut was bad and there was some resistance as he was pushing. It was chipping the melamine surface all the way through the board. He tested again, this time changing the height of the blade. It was even worse. He called his blade sharpening company and told them about the problem. They took it back and discovered the problem. They had accidently sharpened the teeth at an angle that was 3 degrees off the standard. Once they re-sharpened the blade to the correct angle, it cut like butter through the melamine with no chipping.

JUST 3 DEGREES CAN CHANGE EVERYTHING

You may appear to be doing a decent job in your territory, but your numbers are not quite where you want them to be. You push through anyway. You have begun to notice the resistance out there with many accounts. What is it? "Why do I have to work this hard?" It may be because you need to adjust your strategy. Perhaps 3 degrees or 3% in a new direction could change some things. I have given you many ideas to consider. Try a new approach to your daily activities. Always consider that there may be a better way to do what you are doing. Closely look and observe the top sales people in your company. I'm not saying, change everything you are doing, I am saying... make some small adjustments.

Focus on your strengths. You have many attributes that set you apart. Stay positive and be a problem solver for your customers. Be as professional and reliable as you can. Welcome new challenges and stay dedicated. Be a good listener and follow through with your promises.

There is no other job that can give you the freedom and rewards like the profession of selling. It gives you an opportunity to be 'yourself' in front of your customers. It challenges you to be resilient and disciplined. Momentum is hard to start, but it becomes easy to maintain as time passes. There is a big payoff, if you can stick with the job long enough to breathe, and get nice orders that come easier and easier over time. You will begin to love your customers and develop long lasting relationships that make the job even better. It's the relationships that give the huge pay-off. You are given a chance to interact with many different types of people. It's fascinating to be able to see, how some businesses operate and see how things are made.

Don't brag to your company employees about your income or the fact that you get to get out of the office. They will begin to resent you for it. You can remind them of the challenges you face on a daily basis. Outside sales looks so easy and fun from the inside, but it is a hard job to master. Find the right company to work for, with the right products to sell and you will be set. Make certain when you apply for the job, it's not them interviewing you but you interviewing them. You want your work environment to be a 'good fit' for everyone.

I could have never survived outside selling for as long as I have without my faith in God. All the challenges and successes have been a blessing from above. I do not know how anyone can survive the ups and downs of life without faith in a higher power. Believe in God. Pursue God. Learn why so many people that have achieved such great things have had their faith to carry them thru. Act like a PRO, think like a PRO, live like a PRO.

ABOUT THE AUTHOR

Larry Lockshaw began his career working for an engineering firm in Santa Ana, California as a Purchasing Specialist. After 5 years of learning the trade he was given the opportunity to work with a growing company that would put him in an outside sales position. After 9 months of product knowledge training, he was given a territory in San Diego, California. He dedicated himself to the job for a total of 18 years.

With his desire for new challenges, he moved on to explore outside sales positions with other distribution companies. His passion and devotion to outside selling has been the key to his success for over 30 years.

SELLING AT THE PRO LEVEL

REFERENCES

"Employ your time in improving yourself by other men's writings, so that you shall gain easily what others have labored hard for."   - Socrates

'Once at the heart of the US consumer experience, the ubiquitous mall is in crisis. Of 1,200 across the country, just 50% are expected to be in business by 2023' theguardian.com/us-news/2017/jul/22/mall-of-america-minnesota-retail-anniversary

"The quality of a person's life is in direct proportion to their commitment to excellence, regardless of their chosen field of endeavor."   — Vince Lombardi

"Successful people do the things that unsuccessful people are unwilling to do."
— John C. Maxwell

A recent survey revealed, a whopping 55% of sales reps don't have the right skills to be successful. (the Brevet Group) www.thebrevetgroup.com/21-mind-blowing-sales-stats

"The difference between ordinary and extraordinary is that little extra."—Jimmy Johnson, Head coach, Dallas Cowboys (1989-93), Miami Dolphins (1996-99)

"A man must be big enough to admit his mistakes, smart enough to profit from them, and strong enough to correct them."   – John C. Maxwell

30-50% Of Sales Go To The Vendor That RespondsFirst!thebrevetgroup.com/21-mind-blowing-sales-stats

"If it is easy, then you are doing it wrong." -- Gabby Williams, guard, UConn basketball team.

"Confidence comes from being prepared."   -John Wooden

"Never let the fear of striking out get in your way."   -- Babe Ruth, seven-time World Series champion.

"The difference between a successful person and others is not a lack of strength, not a lack of knowledge, but rather in a lack of will."   -Vince Lombardi

SELLING AT THE PRO LEVEL

92% of salespeople give up after no sales on the 4th call. 60% of customers say no four times before saying yes. nugrowth.com/wp-content/uploads/2015/03/NuGrowth_SalesStats_0315

"You will always miss 100 percent of the shots you don't take." -- Wayne Gretzky, Canadian hockey player and leading scorer in NHL history.

Only 13% of customers believe a salesperson can understand their needs.thebrevetgroup.com /21-mind-blowing-sales-stats

86% of customers will pay more for a better customer experience. https://www.groovehq.com/support/customer-service-statistics

67% said they would be willing to pay more money to get same-day delivery. http://www.supplychainquarterly.com/news/20161004-survey-online-shopper--demand-visibility-as-well-as-speed-in-delivery/

44% said Fast Delivery would motivate them to give repeat business. http://www.supplychainquarterly.com/news/20161004-survey-online-shopper--demand-visibility-as-well-as-speed-in-delivery/

According to a report published by Global Entrepreneurship 2015/2016 by Babson College, Over 50% of businesses discontinue operations because of lack of profits or financial funding.   babson.edu/news-events/babson-news/Pages/1-19-12globalgem

A study published in 2014 by the Turnaround Management Society reveals that 54.6% of business crises are caused by the mistakes of top management. The most prominent causes of a crisis are that the management continued with a strategy that was no longer working for the company. They lost touch with the market and their customers and did not want to adapt to changes occurring around them.

Why do Companies fail? 2014 Survey Results, Turnaround Management Society, 14 February 2014

The Bureau of Labor Statistics, Business Employment Dynamics says, around 50% of all businesses no longer exist after 5 years. Only one-third make it past their 10th anniversary.

89% of consumers have stopped doing business with a company after experiencing poor customer service.   slideshare.net/Right Now/2011-customer-experience-impact-report

"The world is run by those who show up"   -Unknown

"The world is run by those who show up"
http://www.barrypopik.com/index.php/new_york_city/entry/the_world_is_run_by_those_who_show_up/

Each year the average business loses approximately 14% of their customers.
https://www.linkedin.com/pulse/each-year-youll-lose-14-your-customers-rotha-chan [Source: BusinessBrief.com] also https://blog.hubspot.com/sales/sales-statistics

Nearly 70 percent of customers leave as a result of their dissatisfaction with the 'business attitude' http://www.americanexecutivecenters.com/why-your-customers-leave/

76% of consumers say they view customer service as the true test of how much a company values them.   – Aspect Consumer Experience Survey

http://www.business2community.com/strategy/6-times-expensive-win-new-customer-retain-existing-one-01483871#sy0hMYJyMDHOmusS.99

It is 6 Times more expensive to win a new customer than to retain an existing one.

http://www.business2community.com/strategy/6-times-expensive-win-new-customer-retain-existing-one-01483871#sy0hMYJyMDHOmusS.99

Email is 40 times more effective at getting new customers than Facebook and Twitter combined. — McKinsey   http://www.mckinsey.com/business-functions/marketing-and-sales

35% of email recipients open email based on the subject line and nothing else. Source: http://sumo.ly/4Cye

80% of calls go to voicemail, and 90% of first-time voicemails are never returned. ringlead.com/25-sales-outreach-statistics-help-sell-better

98% of the top sales professionals say 'relationships' are the most important part of generating new business.   www.business2community.com/social-selling/4-surprising-social-selling-stats-might-change-sales-strategy

Even a fish wouldn't get into trouble if it kept its mouth shut. – Unknown

You can't teach people to be lazy –   either they have it, or they don't.   -Dagwood Bumstead

Nearly 80 percent of Americans are living paycheck to paycheck.   - CareerBuilder. http://www.newsmax.com/Newsfront/americans-live-paycheck-to-paycheck/2017/08/24/id/809486/

SELLING AT THE PRO LEVEL

You will never find yourself at the top of Mt. Everest by accident. – Larry Lockshaw

Success is not the result of spontaneous combustion. You must set yourself on fire.
-Fred Shero   Legendary NHL hockey coach

He who guards his mouth and his tongue keeps himself from calamity. (Proverbs 21:23)

89 percent of consumers turn to Google, Bing or another search engine to find information on products, services or businesses prior to making purchases

Fleishman-Hillard International Communications
fleishmanhillard.com/2012/01/31/2012-digital-influence-index-shows-internet-as-leading-influence-in-consumer-purchasing-choices/

The only thing you can really control is how you react to things out of your control.
-Anonymous

When you're good at making excuses, it's hard to excel at anything else. -John L. Mason

Better three hours too soon, than one minute too late.   -William Shakespeare

Ecommerce is growing 23% year-over-year, yet 46% of American small businesses do not have a website. https://www.bigcommerce.com/blog/ecommerce-trends/

You know you are no longer #1, when you begin to smell like #2.- Mike Daugherty

If you liked this book please share your experience at Amazon

You can contact me at:

GreatAchieversPublishing@gmail.com

SELLING AT THE PRO LEVEL

www.ingramcontent.com/pod-product-compliance
Lightning Source LLC
Chambersburg PA
CBHW020649220526
45464CB00001B/351